Albert Leffingwell

Rambles through Japan without a Guide

Albert Leffingwell
Rambles through Japan without a Guide
ISBN/EAN: 9783744727921
Printed in Europe, USA, Canada, Australia, Japan
Cover: Foto ©Andreas Hilbeck / pixelio.de

More available books at **www.hansebooks.com**

RAMBLES THROUGH JAPAN
WITHOUT A GUIDE.

BY

"ALBERT TRACY."

(pseud.)

Albert (T.) Leffingwell, M.D.

LONDON:
SAMPSON LOW, MARSTON & COMPANY
LIMITED,
St. Dunstan's House,
FETTER LANE, FLEET STREET, E.C.
1892.

PREFACE.

WHAT would happen to a traveller who should find himself alone in the very heart of a "heathen country" like Japan, without knowing a dozen words of the native language? If there is any novelty in the following pages, it is the response they afford to such an inquiry. Innumerable are the volumes written about Japanese life, manners, and customs; but, so far as the writer is aware, no other traveller has made the experiment of plunging into the interior, with no more acquaintance with the speech of the people than may be picked up during a fortnight at the capital, and journeying from one end of the empire to the other, with neither interpreter nor guide.

The notes taken during a three months' ramble have been closely followed, in place of a more carefully prepared and continuous narrative. Written by many instalments during each day, wherever a halt was made for rest—at wayside tea-houses, on the steps of a temple, or at the foot of a shrine, in the midst, oftentimes, of a multitude of eager and curious faces—such a record of experience is rather a series of mental photographs of things as they were seen, than the more carefully toned picture which unaided memory would probably have painted at a later date.

It has the disadvantage not only of unavoidable egotism in expression, but also of occasional repetitions; for more than once the same peculiar incident or curious custom was seen and noted down. Some historical references here and there have been slightly amplified from the original memoranda; the last two or three chapters are condensed from the diary; and some of the latest facts in regard to its public affairs have been added, as of value to every one interested in the gradual development of the country and its progressive transformation.

The writer confesses to regarding Japanese life and manners as a phase of a real civilization; differing very widely indeed from that which has moulded Europe;

doubtless, on the whole, inferior to ours, but nevertheless a civilization as distinct from semi-barbarism as it is possible to conceive. It has so effectually permeated all classes of society, that courtesy and gentle manners everywhere prevail, and a boor is unknown. If Japanese civilization has erred by inculcating an inordinate veneration for antiquity, it has thereby inspired a reverence for authority which might well induce the envy of many a European government. Although Buddhism may be "an outworn creed," it has at least served to prepare for the reception of a better, by creating a population more considerate of each other's rights and privileges than many another even in the Christian world. It is the ambition of Japan now to take her place free and unfettered by the side of other nations. In the end she will undoubtedly succeed. A recent English writer on Japanese affairs, well informed by long residence in the country, tells us that, in common with every Eastern nation, Japan knows well enough that "our Christian and humanitarian professions are 'nothing but bunkum;'" that the history of Egypt and India—and he might have added, of China—"is no secret;" that her people would indeed be blind if they failed to see that their only safety lies in the endeavour to be strong. Well, as Japan exchanges, one by one, the old ideals for the new, let us hope she may cling still to some which are associated with all that is noble in her venerable past; to that sense of honour and that gentle courtesy which have inspired her greatest names; and to that respect for right, founded on justice rather than force, which is the essence, not indeed of our present civilization, but of something better and far more permanent—of Christianity itself.

OXFORD, 1892.

CONTENTS.

CHAPTER I.
ARRIVAL IN JAPAN.

Off the coast—Our fellow-passengers—Yokohama—Stroll in the Japanese quarter—Bastile Day celebrated—Chinese in Yokohama—Their self-importance—The crossing of races—Honour or dishonour? 1

CHAPTER II.
IN AND ABOUT TOKIO.

Comparison with Rome—City of magnificent distances—The jinrikisha-man—A visit to temples—The story of the forty-nine ronins—Japanese honour satisfied—Dinner at a Tokio restaurant—Difference of tastes—The children of the country—A brave boy 11

CHAPTER III.
AN EXCURSION IN THE COUNTRY.

An experimental trip—A morning ride—Luncheon at Ichakawa—Wayside tea-houses—Yawata—Superstition—First night at a Japanese country inn—A bath under difficulties 2

CHAPTER IV.

SAKURA.

A miserable night—Midnight feasts—Arrival at Sakura—The story of Sogoro—A martyr deified—Homeward bound—Second night's experience—Entertainment at supper—Arrival at Tokio 29

CHAPTER V.

A PILGRIMAGE TO NIKKO.

Excursion with a guide—The flea-bag—The Mikado's soldiers—A Buddhist subscription-list—Telegraphs and idols—Oyama silk-weaving—A girl at the loom—Wonders of an opera-glass—The great avenue of trees—Arrival at Nikko 38

CHAPTER VI.

NIKKO AND ITS SHRINES.

Temple architecture compared—Mausoleums and shrines—The Buddhist saint—The Assisi of Japan—Tomb of Iye-yasu—Pilgrim devotions—Nikko's ruins—Statues of Amida—Waku's desecration—Return journey—" Foreign accommodation "—Arrival at Tokio 47

CHAPTER VII.

PLANS AND PREPARATIONS.

The route decided—The mountain road—Decision to go alone—Disadvantages of being " personally conducted "—The " squeezing " process universal—Note for future excursionists 60

CHAPTER VIII.

OVERLAND TOWARD KIOTO.

PAGE

A midnight start—Inquisitive fellow-passengers—Honjo—
Stroll about the town—Prevalence of blindness—School
children—The silk industry—Japanese bargains—Village
industries—Crossing the Umezawa Pass—Arrival at
Ozawa 65

CHAPTER IX.

A CROSS-COUNTRY EXCURSION.

Ironworks at Ozawa—A Japanese engineer—Exploration of
a mine—First ride on native pony—Mio-gi-san—Attempts
at conversation—Rustic bridges—Spiders and leeches—
On the Naka-sen-do—Over Usui pass—Karuizawa—
Chanting pilgrims 84

CHAPTER X.

ON THE NAKA-SEN-DO.

Pilgrims and prayers—Supplications for a penny—Oiwake by
coach—Provoking experiences—Apparently a mirage—
Mochidzuke—Fun at my expense—The long Wada pass
—New costumes—Shimo no Suwa—Japanese dogs—
Inherent gentleness of the people—A pious landlord ... 100

CHAPTER XI.

THE MOUNTAIN REGION.

The Shiwo-jiri Pass—Peculiar house architecture—A country
bridge—Visit to Matsumoto—An inhospitable town—
Return to Shiwo-jiri—Walk to Niyegawa—Mysteries of

a magnifying-glass—Letter of introduction given—Hirosawa—Picturesque village—Singular female costume—Village industries—Beasts of burden 117

CHAPTER XII.

IN THE HEART OF JAPAN.

Agematsu—Magnificent scenery—Mountain mills—Village processions and dancing dragons—The artist in dough—Call from the schoolmaster—Lightning rods upon telegraph-poles—At whose suggestion?—Isumago—Magome Pass—On a pack-horse—A narrow bridge—Led by a woman—Oi—Comforts of Japanese inns 133

CHAPTER XIII.

MITAKE TO OTSU.

Across the Kisogawa—Bridge-building—Melons—Gifu and its silks—Seki-ga-hara—Akasaka—An honest friend—Samegai—Same inventions from universal needs—Lake Biwa—Steamboat to Otsu—Mi-i-dera monastery—A Japanese Samson—Ben-kei's giant soup-kettle 157

CHAPTER XIV.

KIOTO.

The ancient capital—Resemblance to Philadelphia—Deified statesmen—Temples—Nan-zen-ji monastery—The thousand images of Kwannon—The great bell—Cyclopian masonry—Temple of Kiyomidzu-dera—The sin-cleansing fountain—Nude sinners—Young Japan 171

CHAPTER XV.

THE CITY OF PEACE.

The mikado's palace—City hospital—Shimo-gamo temple—A freak of nature—Odd ceremonies—Temple of Nishi-hon-gwan-ji—Buddhist prayer-meeting—A youthful abbot—Chi-on-in monastery—Relics of antiquity—A manuscript fifteen centuries old—Musical floor—Stone Age in Japan—Kioto by night 186

CHAPTER XVI.

NARA AND KO-YA-SAN.

An inland excursion—Tea plantations—A stray Chinaman—Midnight alarms—Uji—Nara—An ancient city—A pagoda older than Westminster Abbey—The Dai-Butsu—The great bell—Votive offerings—A picture of terror—Saint Ko-bo Dai-shi—The holy mountain of Ko-ya-san—Hospitable monks... 206

CHAPTER XVII.

OZAKA.

Descent of Ko-ya-san—Travelling acrobats—Sakai—Ozaka—The "Take-shiki-ya"—The castle of Ozaka—Stones twenty feet long—A September cyclone—Hotel tied down—River scenes—American missionaries—Calling upon converts—A Christian service—Japan already more than half Christian 227

CHAPTER XVIII.

ON THE INLAND SEA.

A native steamboat—Night voyage—Primitive accommodation—" Boy ! "—Okayama—The American mission—

xiv   *Contents.*

PAGE

Call upon the governor—A Buddhist's praise of Christianity—A Japanese prison visited—On the Inland Sea—Islands and villages—Disembarking in darkness—A solitary sail—Unpleasant apprehensions—Night ride in a jinrikisha—Arrival at Hiroshima 250

CHAPTER XIX.

HIROSHIMA TO NAGASAKI.

About Hiroshima—Hospital and schools—Call from the governor—Excursion to Miyajima—Fifteen miles at a stretch—Antiquities and relics—Dinner and poetry—Longest jinrikisha journey—Shimonoseki—Scene of the bombardment—The story of a wrong—Opinion of Sir E. J. Reed, M.P.—Voyage to Nagasaki—Last day in Japan—Steamships coaled by children—Off for China ... 259

CHAPTER XX.

THE PRESENT AND FUTURE OF JAPAN.

Statistics of population—Comparison with England—Death-rates—Physicians and hospitals—Marriage and divorce—Foreign residents—The work of the missionary—A laudable ignorance—Commercial ideals—European policy in the Orient—Lord Elgin on the war in China—The entanglement of Japan by treaty—Opinion of General Grant—His advice—The hope for the future 270

NOTE   286

LIST OF ILLUSTRATIONS.

	PAGE
THE ROAD TO NIKKO	*Frontispiece*
YOKOHAMA	6
AN ANGLO-JAPANESE GIRL	9
TOKIO	17
TEMPLE AT NIKKO	49
A MORNING CALL	72
THE WAYSIDE INN	98
A JAPANESE PEASANT	114
A BUDDHIST TEMPLE, KIOTO	174
THE GREAT BELL	179
A WINTER COSTUME	193
A JAPANESE THEATRE	202
A JAPANESE GIRL	228
A STREET IN OZAKA	244
A SOUTHERN JINRIKISHA	264

"A perfectly paternal government, a perfectly filial people, a community entirely self-supporting, peace within and without, no want, no ill-will between classes,—this is what I find in Japan in the year 1858, *after one hundred years' exclusion of foreigners and foreign trade. Twenty years hence, what will be the contrast?*

" . . . God grant that in opening their country to the West we may not be bringing upon them misery and ruin."— LETTERS OF LORD ELGIN, *during his mission to Japan* (1858).

RAMBLES THROUGH JAPAN
WITHOUT A GUIDE.

CHAPTER I.

ARRIVAL IN JAPAN.

Off the coast—Our fellow-passengers—Yokohama—Stroll in the Japanese quarter—Bastile Day celebrated—Chinese in Yokohama—Their self-importance—The crossing of races—Honour or dishonour?

S.s. *City of Pekin*, *July* 10.—We reach Japan to-morrow, the captain tells us. It has been the shortest passage on record, and with very little of interest to break the monotony of a long sea voyage. The Pacific has been worthy of its name. As we left the harbour of San Francisco the Chinese sailors climbed into the rigging and scattered bits of gilt tissue paper to the winds. We were told they were prayers to the Chinese Neptune for a good voyage. The result has undoubtedly increased faith in the god of storms, for we have had favourable winds every day.

There are only twelve first-class passengers—all men. Three are naval officers, going out to their ships in China seas; two are Japanese merchants established in New York, returning home to make purchases; two or three are Americans engaged in business in Yokohama; one is a missionary bound for China; and the rest of us are "globe-trotters." The principal amusement during the voyage has been gambling, which has gone on from 9 a.m. till midnight, Sundays *not* excepted. The players have settled up their accounts, and I understand the chief winners are two young men, just graduated from Oxford, who were taught the game since coming aboard! Great is the disgust of the Americans who invited them to take a hand, and volunteered to "teach them the game."

The evening is beautiful, the air soft, balmy, and the sea stirred only enough to break into a shimmering path the reflection of the full moon in the water. Somehow every one seems more quiet than usual; thoughts stray homeward. "I would give almost anything to have my wife with me such an evening as this," said the naval captain. He has left his family in San Francisco—four little children, and no chance or hope of seeing them for three years to come. "I don't think of it; I *can't* think of it; I must think only of each day's duties as they come to me. We understood what it was to be when we entered the service, or," he added, after a pause, "at least we thought we understood it."

Our Japanese passengers are very pleasant, and have told me a great deal about the customs of the people. There is no difficulty whatever, they say, in travelling alone about the country, except ignorance of the language. I have already learned from them how to count—the first lesson of civilization.

Yokohama, July 11.—The firing of a cannon over my head at three o'clock this morning announced to the inhabitants the arrival of our steamer.

At break of day I went on deck to get that first view of Japan which so charms and surprises all who see it for the first time. All about the ship were little unpainted boats, whose owners were eager to land passengers for a sixpence; but with the ignorance of a stranger I preferred awaiting the arrival of the steam-launch sent out by the different hotels. On reaching shore, found good quarters at the Grand Hotel; and have spent the day in obtaining impressions and mental photographs.

One cannot readily forget the first day in a new land. Everything is strange; trifles are amusing. Leaving the principal street and eluding jinrikisha-men—more persistent even than Neapolitan hackmen—I found my way on foot to the Japanese town.

In Asia at last! Everything is new, strange, different. All the houses are unpainted; storm and sunshine have given them a rich greyish-brown tint, the natural hue of unstained wood. The ground-floor, a shop usually, is sometimes open to the street, sometimes half-shaded by a bamboo screen. Every device seems to have the purpose of letting in the air and keeping out the sunlight.

A bookseller's shop was the scene of my first purchase. One sits down on the doorstep, or the counter, or the floor—they are much the same. The proprietor leaves his work at the back of the shop, and, coming forward, drops on his knees and bows profoundly. I return the salute after the manner of my people. A pause ensues. There is difficulty in beginning a conversation. Opening a book, I point to the pictures; he comprehends, and brings me a selection of his wares. After choosing a few, I spring upon him one of the very few Japanese words I picked up on the voyage—" Ikura?" or "How much is this?" He answers in one of the tongues of Babel! Somehow I do not catch his meaning as well as he understands mine; and yet I thought I knew how to count in Japanese. "Ikura?" I say again. A profound bow, and the same unmeaning words. How stupid a strange language sounds! I look reflective, as if studying the question from a mercenary standpoint, and slowly shake my head. He is respectful, but firm. Over the face of his wife I fancy a smile crept, as if she penetrated my absolute ignorance. Finally I take a bit of paper and make signs for him to write down the price,

Arrival in Japan. 5

which he does—in Chinese! However, I give him a bit of money, out of which he returns such a surprisingly large amount of change that I fear he has made a mistake in calculating. 'Tis no time for explanations. We part with distinguished salutations.

Across the street is a photographer. His negatives in frames lean against the steps outside, or wherever a bit of sunlight can be had. Here I am more fortunate as to conversation; his replies to my "Ikura?" I really understand. Photographs are always of interest, and his are surprisingly cheap—a penny each. As my purchase seems likely to be considerable for him, he determines to treat, and sending out a servant, she returns with two glasses of iced-water, which we drink to our better acquaintance. A crowd gathers about the door, the eager jinrikisha-man, idle apprentices, young girls with babies strapped on their backs. It would seem that even in Yokohama the stray foreigner is something of a curiosity. How courteous and polite these shopkeepers are! Paris even is outdone. But, then, it is never very difficult to spend money, whether or not one knows the language.

Yokohama, July 14.—This appears to be a general holiday. Flags everywhere are flying, the banks are closed, and business generally suspended. Why? Simply because a hundred years ago a people, rising *en masse*, attacked a fortress; that, and the events that followed, make the day memorable. Is anything more singular

YOKOHAMA.

than the importance which history, looking backward, assigns to events that seemed even to observers of but transitory significance? Of that patriotic mob which poured into the Bastile when at last it surrendered, was there one who could have dreamed that a century afterwards, on shores where the very name of France was then unknown, that deed and that day would be remembered with honour and pride?

I notice quite a colony of Chinese here in Yokohama, and of a type decidedly different from those one sees in California, where for the most part they are servants and labourers, "hewers of wood and drawers of water." Here many of them seem to be fairly well-to-do merchants and money-changers. Clothed in silk and fine linen, they are of a higher caste every way than the Hongkong or Canton coolie who finds his way to the States. One gets accustomed to the supercilious, half-concealed contempt of a San Francisco laundry-man, who condescends to do up the barbarian's linen; but the national satisfaction with themselves seems infinitely more marked in these sleek, smooth-faced Tartars who change your money. Their position in the bank seems to be fairly secure. I was told the other day, that not long ago one of these *compradores*, or money-changers, attached to one of the principal banks, insulted the manager, and was bundled off the premises. The next day their bills were refused at every money-changer's office in the city; the day after, every merchant begged his customer to pay some other currency; and the third day the bank surrendered, and reinstated their compradore. Evidently they are strong in their position here. Out of his own country the Chinaman is like the Jew. You may dislike him, but you cannot dispense with his services. He returns scorn for scorn, and our Western pride with unspeakable contempt.

It is always unsafe to draw one's conclusions respecting a country from the character of a seaport population. The "globe-trotter" who judges Japan from Yokohama is as wise as the Oriental pilgrim who should picture English society from his chance experience in Glasgow or Liverpool, or judge American morality solely by rambles in New York and New Orleans. The intermingling in commercial relations of Occidental and Oriental races seems everywhere in Asia to create a new theory of morals. What would be regarded decidedly wrong at home looks right enough in Asia. One gentleman, for many years a resident in Yokohama, told me that in every one of the new treaty ports a new race is growing up, corresponding with the Eurasian of British India. Every foreigner engaged in commercial pursuits, is expected, if he has no family at home, to take a Japanese wife. I say "wife," because, as in the State of New York, no religious ceremony is necessary to make the relation quite legal, according to Japanese law. But supposing the merchant retires from business? Then he "divorces" his wife; provides for her future, and that of her children, if she has any; and sails away to European respectability. Sometimes he departs without making any provision for his offspring, and leaving their mother to poverty. Still, as the relation, in Japanese eyes, is a sort of wedlock, her reputation is in no way injured, nor her chances diminished of making another marriage.

Everywhere in and about the European quarter I came upon children of the mixed race, some of them exceedingly good-looking. About one I was told a little history that perhaps points a moral, unforeseen by impetuous youth.

AN ANGLO-JAPANESE GIRL.

Some years ago a young man came to Japan to seek his fortune, and in a short time had followed the example of his friends and compatriots in setting up his household gods. Two children were born to him—"the handsomest children in Yokohama," said his friend, who told me the story. Fortune favoured, and the young adventurer was taken into partnership, and rapidly acquired a fortune. At last he returns for a visit to his native land. "Why doesn't he marry and take his wife back to Japan?" is the general inquiry of intimate friends. It would seem to be a very natural proceeding. He can divorce his Japanese wife, according to Jewish customs, by simply sending her home to her parents. But the children? He loves them; he is proud of them. How shall he introduce them to his new wife? Life goes well enough as it is. The mother of his children is gentle, obedient, faithful, although she will never be seen or heard of outside Japan. He will not marry. He returns to Japan, uncertain, perhaps, whether to be discontented or satisfied, and life goes on as before. Some day he will die. She will be provided for; and his children, receiving a European education, will inherit a good share of what he leaves behind. Outside Asia, no one will guess what mingled currents of blood course through their veins.

I am far from being certain that his decision is to be condemned. He might have acted with meanness and dishonour, retaining nevertheless the good opinion of the world—satisfied to be ignorant. For I am told that cases have been known where men, who have acquired a fortune on these shores, have returned home to Europe and America, leaving even daughters behind them, without the least provision for their education or future support. And to what a fate!

CHAPTER II.

IN AND ABOUT TOKIO.

Comparison with Rome—City of magnificent distances—The jinrikisha-man—A visit to temples—The story of the forty-nine ronins—Japanese honour satisfied—Dinner at a Tokio restaurant—Difference of tastes—The children of the country—A brave boy.

Tokio, July 19.—It is a little singular that to me Tokio constantly suggests a comparison with modern Rome. The differences are great, but so are the similitudes. The same brown skins, and variegated costumes of country folk; the same love of sunshine and half-nudity; the narrow streets; the careless poverty that sleeps by the wayside at midday; the shorn and shaven priests; the crowded temples; the heights and intervening valleys —all these bring to mind the ancient capital of the world. Then, too, Rome is here suggested by the same desire of the inhabitants for new buildings, and by the intermingling of town and country within the city limits.

Fifteen years ago one could start from the Colosseum and wander for hours through by-paths and vineyards with nothing to suggest that he was bounded by the walls of imperial Rome. So with Tokio. Outside the centre and business part of the capital the greater portion seems to consist of villages, quite distinct from one another, yet together constituting one metropolis, much perhaps as if London, a century ago, had then embraced the town it now includes.

Tokio is a city of magnificent distances, and the jinrikisha has been in great request. Of all methods of conveyance this is the most convenient. Riding at full speed, you can draw up in an instant, and that by a word. My karuma-man is a stout, comical-looking fellow, good natured and willing, and as strong as a horse. Besides a blue shirt, he wears only a pair of cotton drawers ending above the knee, and a blue handkerchief twisted or knotted round his head. Turning corners, his deep guttural "hei! hei!" sends all foot-passengers scattering to the side of the road, along which he rushes at full speed. We seem constantly in danger of collision with other jinrikishas of the same kind, but nothing of the sort happens; perhaps even horses would be careful if they owned the carriages to which they are attached. These jinrikishas or karumas appear to be used by all classes. Sometimes one would imagine that even beggars are riding, only in this country bare legs are no certain sign of poverty.

I have visited the temples : all interesting, but chiefly for the crowds which frequent them. Mothers bring their little ones, and put their tiny palms together in the attitude of reverence or prayer, as they face the image of the merciful goddess, Kwan-non. Before each temple or shrine is the inevitable money-box; here often a huge wooden chest, into which, through oblique slits, the grateful worshipper throws his coppers. One of these chests was at least six or eight feet in length.

At the temple of Sen-gaku-ji are to be seen the graves of the forty-nine ronins, the story of whose vengeance and voluntary death is one, not only of great dramatic interest, but most significant of Japanese character. It seems that in the year 1701 a certain nobleman of high rank, being grossly insulted by another, drew his sword with the purpose of avenging the indignity offered him. Unfortunately for him, this outburst of passion happened within the very palace of the Shogun, where to unsheathe a weapon in anger was a capital offence. No palliation was possible, and it was hinted to the offender that he was expected with as little delay as possible to perform hara-kiri, which he accordingly did.

But this by no means accorded with the ideas of justice held by his retainers. Their master was dead; the man who insulted him lived. They plotted to obtain revenge; even though each one of them knew that his own death would immediately follow. After

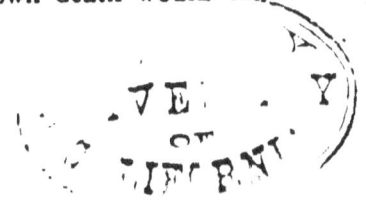

more than a year spent in absence from the capital, and in allaying all suspicion of danger, on the night of January 30, 1703, the conspirators made their attack on the house of their lord's foe. Dragging him from his hiding-place, they informed him that his last hour had come; giving him, however, the opportunity of dying honourably by "happy despatch." Their courtesy does not appear to have been duly appreciated, for in the end they were obliged to cut off his head. Leaving the house, they made their way to their master's grave, and kneeling about it, deposited thereon the head of his foe. Not one of them seems to have thought of personal safety or of possible escape. But if honour must be satisfied, crime must also be punished, and each man suffered the penalty of death.

Here, in a little cemetery in suburban Tokio, I visited their graves. Each has its own head-stone; they are grouped about the tomb of their lord and master, to revenge whose untimely death each man gave up his life. A like history I do not believe is to be found in the records of any other nation. While I was there, more than one pilgrim, foot-sore and travel-stained, entered the enclosure and knelt for a moment of prayer or invocation before each grave. For nearly two hundred years, then, this has been sacred to memory of men who loved the honour of their lord better than their own lives. At such a shrine, for what, I wonder, do these pilgrims pray? For as keen a sense of honour? For

In and about Tokio.

fidelity as sure? Or for loaves and fishes, for hidden treasure, or success in trade? I hope the first.

Dined yesterday with my two Japanese fellow-voyagers from San Francisco. "Before trying to travel through the country," said Mr. Sato, "you should have one good dinner in real Japanese style, for you get no idea of our cookery at your hotel." A few minutes' walk brought us to one of the principal restaurants in Tokio, and in the outer court we were met by the proprietor with profoundest salutations. Removing shoes and sandals, we went upstairs, and were ushered into a room perfectly plain and empty. One end looked out upon a tiny garden; I say "end," because the entire side of the house seemed taken out. The floor was spread with clean matting, upon which, in the centre of the room, were four circular bits of oil-cloth, about a yard in diameter. "Will you be seated?" cried my friend, who had many a laugh at my ineffectual efforts to double into any comfortable position on a floor—a thing I gave up utterly—assuming, instead, a half-reclining posture. In front of each guest was a tray upon which was a carven section of bamboo, fashioned so as to be a receptacle for smoked-out tobacco, and beside it an earthen bowl with live coals, covered thinly with ashes, fantastically arranged in shape of a volcano, and used to light pipe or cigar. The tobacco smoked is very mild, and the custom is to take but three or four whiffs at a time.

The host clapped his hands; a serving-maid came, who, dropping upon her knees, bent her head to the floor to hear our august wishes, and then disappeared. Returning, she brought us tea in the smallest of cups, accompanied with confectionery, sprinkled with powdered tea-leaves. These are brought in before every meal; whether luncheon, dinner, or breakfast, one always has tea and candy. The other dishes were brought on in courses, but not removed during the meal. First came, in blue china bowls, a soup tasting something like the liquor of raw oysters, in which was half the head of a large fish. "Why, it has the eye in it!" I said with a shudder. "The eye is the choice part," said my Japanese friend, extracting this portion of his fish with a chop-stick, and swallowing it with gusto. "They use only the head of the fish, and serve one eye to each guest. Try it; it is delicious." It was *not* delicious to me. The next dish was shreds of raw fish served with a kind of ginger sauce. Poising a bit of the fish between your chop-sticks, you dip it into the sauce and then convey it to your mouth. I did not like it. Something besides fishes' heads or raw fish would have been acceptable. But the next course was fish, cooked; and then a boiled lobster cooked whole, one to each guest; an omelette; and rice eaten without sugar, milk, or any kind of sauce. These, with hot and cold *saké*, completed the repast. There is no grease in the cooking, and very little artificial addition of extraneous flavours. That

TOKIO.

which a Japanese finds most distasteful in European cookery is the greasiness of so many dishes. Said Sato, "Butter and lard seem necessary to your existence; but to me even cheese at first was as horrible as putrid flesh would be to you." *Saké*, the national drink, made from rice, is served in little cups holding about a large tablespoonful.

I half suspect that the first part of the dinner, after all, was no fair example of Japanese hotel cuisine, but contrived for my benefit, and consisting chiefly of unusual dishes. A Frenchman doesn't live on frogs or snails; but he might prepare a dish of both for the benefit of a foreign guest.

The children, it seems to me, must seem charming to every traveller; they are so quiet and pretty and well-behaved—and especially so polite. I amused myself by bowing profoundly to a half-naked youngster; but he returned my salutation gravely, and with equal formality. The younger children are occasionally terrified at sight of me. Perhaps mothers have frightened them into good behaviour by vague hints as to the "hairy-faced foreigner." Many times babies on their mothers' backs break out into violent crying, as they see me looking at them. One morning I came upon a little boy of five or six playing with two younger children in the road. I stopped a moment to look at them, when patting the others on the back with a hurried injunction to get behind him, he faced me with a piteous, scared, but admirably brave look, as if to say, "I don't know what you are going to do; but you can't touch my little brother and sister till you've killed me!" I hope he thought better of me before we parted.

CHAPTER III.

AN EXCURSION IN THE COUNTRY.

An experimental trip—A morning ride—Luncheon at Ichakawa —Wayside tea-houses—Yawata—Superstition—First night at a Japanese country inn—A bath under difficulties.

July 21.—The great trouble in planning for a long trip into the interior is my ignorance of what is really necessary to take with me. Many articles spoken of in the guide-book as absolutely indispensable, are certainly not requisite for my comfort. Why not make a little experimental trip somewhere, and take little or nothing? The idea seemed a good one. So I started this morning on a trip to Sakura, a place about thirty miles from Tokio, the scene of the martyrdom of a Japanese peasant some two and a half centuries ago. Within a day's journey of the capital one ought not to suffer any great risks, even in case of sickness or accident.

As to provisions, I propose to find out exactly what one really needs by taking little or nothing, except two or three loaves of bread. The matter of conveyance was left to the hotel proprietor; he secured a strong young fellow by the name of Matoi, blind in one eye, but with an infinite fund of good nature, and as a rule fairly quick at comprehension of sign-language. Through an interpreter, he has been made to understand the very moderate distance he is to travel every day; and that whenever I repeat the name "Tokio," and point backward in the direction of the capital, he is to turn back directly. Of English he knows not a single word.

Bright and early this morning Matoi made his appearance with a new jinrikisha. My luggage is exceedingly light, consisting only of a small portmanteau; and in ten minutes we were tearing along at a great pace through the clean streets and suburbs of Tokio.

No sooner were we fairly out of town than an unforeseen difficulty occurred. Matoi was made to understand by the hotel manager that I wished to sleep to-night at Usui, a village about twenty-seven miles distant. This is a very moderate run for a good coolie to travel on a level road; and I had calculated upon being there shortly after luncheon, having the afternoon to spend in rambling about the town. Unfortunately, no explanation of this plan of mine was given to the coolie, and he naturally took the day to his work. Immediately after quitting the suburbs of Tokio, through which he rushed faster than a horse would ordinarily travel, he dropped into a good, easy pace, which he rightly calculated would bring him to Usui about six o'clock in the evening, and allow plenty of time for resting at tea-houses along the way. I don't believe he was stupid; but it was impossible to make him comprehend why I wanted to get on faster. One could not apply other than moral suasion to him, and he evidently felt bound merely to get to the destination before night. Why should he try to do more? He didn't understand; and I couldn't explain.

For the first ten miles to the boundary of the treaty limits, beyond which no traveller should go without a passport, the road is rather monotonous. Part of the way it lies along the top of a narrow dyke, in either side of which were patches of rice, green and flourishing. In the muddy slime and swamp produced by irrigation, women were at work weeding, and otherwise cultivating the rice planted in hills or tufts a few inches apart.

The village of Ichakawa was reached a little after eleven o'clock, and stopping before a nice little tea-house overlooking the river, my man intimated by sign-language that he would like to eat. Somehow, none of the numerous dishes appeared very inviting, except the boiled rice; but this seems to be of better quality, and better cooked, than I have ever seen it elsewhere. A little maid seated herself before me with a large wooden bucket filled with steaming rice, and filling my bowl with the contents, replaced the cover, and waited till a new supply was asked for. All other dishes seem merely con-

An Excursion in the Country.

diments for the rice. The attendants were pretty, and charmingly dressed; and every one in the house, sooner or later, found opportunity to enter the room, drop on his or her knees, and gaze with great wondering eyes at the bearded foreigner. Certainly my charioteer appeared to enjoy his dinner, for he ate with gusto all of the luxuries provided for both of us; but I had no appetite. Of boiled rice, some dry bread, and a little tea, I made my first dinner at a native inn.

The ferry across the river was a primitive but safe affair; it consisted of a large flat-bottomed boat, unpainted, and propelled by a long bamboo pole in the hands of a stout peasant. The ferryman's price could hardly be called extortionate; to carry my vehicle and luggage and two passengers to the other side of the river, he asked three sen, or about a penny!

We had now passed beyond treaty limits, into a district rarely visited by foreigners. There is not much in the scenery to attract; but to me everything is novel and interesting. A tendency to nudity appears more frequent as one leaves Tokio behind; we encounter children of both sexes, even up to six or seven years of age, absolutely naked, making mud-pies by the wayside, or chasing each other about the street. At work, a simple cloth about the loins was the only garment of the labourer, or even of the lounging traveller at the wayside inn. I came across one old man, a pilgrim, resting for a while under a tree, whose entire body was tattooed with pictures of dragons, tigers, and every kind of imaginable beast. Descending from the karuma, and approaching him for a nearer view, he very hurriedly robed himself in a blue cotton gown, and started off as if greatly frightened. Doubtless he mistook me for some government official, stopping my journey to arrest him for law-breaking. It is strictly against the law to go thus scantily clad; but one can hardly hope to change by a stroke of a pen a natural custom, to which for centuries the people have been inured. In Tokio, at least, the law seems very strictly enforced.

All along the roadside, about a mile apart, one comes upon little resting-places for travellers to take tea; booths of bamboo, generally in front of a straw-thatched cottage, with a peasant proprietor. At one of these booths, kept by a girl perhaps twenty years of age, we made our next stopping-place. The fair proprietress was quite pretty, notwithstanding blackened teeth, which a little detracted from her good looks. It is a mistake, I was recently told, to conclude that only married women stain their teeth; it is a fashion without uniformity of adherence. The hostess bustled about, bringing to me assorted specimens of native confectionery—rather tasteless, by the way—and serving tea which she had made as we approached. Matoi, who had disappeared to give himself the luxury of a shower-bath at the well, came round while I was eating, looking very ruddy and refreshed, and, seating himself on a bench, sipped his tea without the least apparent consciousness that he was as naked as Adam—at least after the fall. The girl was a regular little flirt; for having with much pantomime induced me to give her one of the sweetmeats, she wrapped it in rice paper, and put it away in her bosom, pretending she meant to keep it as a souvenir. A button of my coat being loose, she noticed it, and producing needle and thread, sewed it on again with many questionings meantime, and little laughs at my inability to comprehend. When finally we took our departure, her "Sa-yo-na-ra" followed us along the road.

The afternoon journey was through a succession of towns and villages all very much alike. At Yawata, a peasant village close by the roadside, is a small grove of bamboos, into which the country people for centuries were afraid to penetrate. There seems to be a tradition that it is haunted by a spirit who objects to trespassers. Many centuries ago a prince, travelling this way, entered this growth, and was suddenly thrown to the earth by some supernatural agency. In 1868 some soldiers seem to have trespassed without incurring any penalty from the guardian demon; and I ventured to penetrate it for about one hundred yards, not accompanied, however, by any of the villagers, who could not be induced to go within the glade. So dense is the shade of the tall bamboos that even at midday the gloom was very great, and one could hardly wonder at the mystery which surrounds the place. In the grounds of a temple near this place is a singular tree about ten feet in diameter, which has the appearance of being composed of many small trees which have grown together. As something out of the line of ordinary vegetation, of course the tree is regarded by the native with becoming reverence.

Descending a rather steep road shortly before sundown, we reached Usui; and I have had my first experience in a native town. The best room was already occupied, but Matoi probably made the innkeeper understand that only the best would suit his employer, for the earlier travellers were obliged to turn out and take an inferior apartment. The room to which I was shown was as beautifully neat and clean as one could wish, but absolutely empty of furniture. No provision exists for private ablutions in sleeping-rooms. Taking a towel, I found my way to the courtyard, and proceeded to rid myself thoroughly of the dust of travel, surrounded by all the domestics of the place. On returning to my room—which commanded a very pretty prospect over a lake—Matoi appeared. He, too, looked refreshed. We entered into conversation, if that can be called converse wherein ideas are chiefly conveyed by signs. Wouldn't I like a regular bath? It struck me favourably. A clean Japanese gown was brought, and, undressing, I put it on, took my night-robe and towels in hand, and followed to the bath-room, where a stout maid was mixing hot and cold water in a square tub.

But, the bath finished, an unforeseen difficulty occurred. Matoi had carried off my Japanese gown, and my own night-robe was white! The idea of walking around a public-house, or even a country inn, arrayed only in a white night-shirt somehow shocked my sense of propriety. I called to Matoi. He came, respectfully bowing. I pointed to my white gown. "Hai," he answered. That means nothing but "Yes." I remonstrated firmly but pointedly. "Hai," he again ejaculates, seemingly puzzled at what I can possibly want. Then he asks me something in Japanese. But I haven't brought my dictionary to the bath-room; I don't know what he means. Seeing I have quite finished bathing, he throws open the door, and makes signs for me to follow him upstairs. A crowd of servants and domestics are waiting to see me come out. There is no help for it—I go. To my surprise, not a soul laughs or seems a particle more astonished at a foreigner in a white robe walking about than if he wore a blue one. And really it was absurd to think that any impropriety pertains merely to the colour of the cloth.

I have finished supper. It was meagre enough for an anchorite; merely bread and rice, with tea and a boiled egg. There was an abundance of other things furnished in little bowls; fish cooked and uncooked; broth of strange odour and mysterious composition, shell-fish, cuttle-fish, and seaweed, all of which I tasted, and turned over to my jinrikisha-man, to his infinite delight. It seemed as if most of the dishes were luxuries to which he was unaccustomed; for even the fragments he gathered up. How curious that articles of food which are an abomination to one human being are so relished by another! Yet everything was good and clean; it was simply strange to me.

Dinner finished, Matoi inquired — by going through the pantomime of closing his eyes and snoring—whether I wished to retire? There was no use standing about in a room without furniture, and I indicated assent. The maid-servant then brought into the chamber three or four thick cotton mattresses, and made a bed on the floor, placing a dainty wooden head-rest at one end; then she stretched over it all a mosquito-net with its corners secured to the sides of the room; and leaving behind her a paper lantern, in which a tiny wick floats upon a basin of oil, she made her final prostration, and left me to my note-book and "what dreams may come."

CHAPTER IV.

SAKURA.

A miserable night—Midnight feasts—Arrival at Sakura—The story of Sogoro—A martyr deified — Homeward bound—Second night's experience — Entertainment at supper — Arrival at Tokio.

July 22.—"I have passed a miserable night," but it was not from "fearful dreams." The very novelty of the situation made sleep impossible. Noisy travellers splashed about in the court below, shouting to servants, or singing snatches of song. The bed on the floor was hard, but the wooden pillow was harder. Finally I discarded it altogether, and improvised a head-rest from my overcoat, tightly rolled, and wrapped in a towel. The night was uncomfortably warm, and the house seemed hermetically sealed. The sliding panels, which, being removed during the day, give such a summer-house appearance to a Japanese residence, were tightly closed. About midnight I could stand it no longer, and opened one of the panels for some fresh air. It creaked so loudly that I fancied myself liable to be taken for a housebreaker.

Then my miserable charioteer kept me awake. Long after midnight I could hear him munching the delicacies he had saved from supper. Then followed a few whiffs from his pipe; ending with little taps of the bamboo pipe-stem against the brazier to knock the ashes from the bowl. A nap of an hour was followed by another midnight feast and another smoke. Has the wretched man no fear of dyspepsia? Finally, when I had dropped into troubled slumbers, it seemed hardly an hour before morning came. Everybody must awake at the same time, it appears. The outer partitions or shutters were taken down; travellers shouted for breakfast; a servant entered my room without ceremony and opened the panels; morning had come. Two minutes after rising, the net and bedding had all been removed to a closet, and the room transformed again into a summer-house. Breakfast was doubtless excellent, but I cared for nothing, after so sleepless a night. Again Matoi revelled in abundance; he fairly beamed with satisfaction and good nature when I paid the bill. How could I have suspected him of a conspiracy with the landlord to "squeeze" me, after such feasting on the very fat of the land?

By six o'clock we were off for Sakura, and in an hour or two I was standing before the monument marking the spot where, nearly two and a half centuries ago, a poor Japanese peasant with his wife and children, were put to death. The story, as told by Mr. Mitford, is one of the most pathetic in the annals of heroism. In 1644 the country-folk of this section were so oppressed by land-agents that their condition became even more unbearable than that of the French peasantry before the Revolution. They had neither newspaper nor Parliament whereby to make known their wrongs, or to seek redress, and every remonstrance was dangerous. Some of them met together one day and determined to send a petition to their feudal lord, the *daimio*, or baron, who spent the money wrung by their taxation and rack-rents in the dissipations of Yedo. Their petition was unheeded, perhaps even unread; and their wrongs seemed without remedy. Moved at last by the great suffering of those about him, Sogoro, a man of middle age, determined, as a last and most desperate resort, to present in person the petition of the oppressed peasantry to his august greatness, the Tycoon. Taking leave of his friends, he went to Yedo, secreted himself under a bridge over which the Shogun was to pass, and at the right time pushed the petition, at the end of a long bamboo, directly into the royal hands!

The indecorum of this act was without parallel in the annals of Japan. A rude and common peasant had forcibly broken down all barriers of etiquette, and disturbed the tranquillity of the great Shogun himself. Inquiry followed. The justice of the peasants' complaints was proven. But in other lands, and at later epochs, the wrongful oppression of rulers has been held to constitute no palliation for the violence of the oppressed. In this case, royal seclusion had been trampled upon, and an example must be made. By orders of the Government, the wrongs of the peasantry appear to have been completely redressed, while, at the same time, by the irony of fate, the one man through whose audacity relief had come, was delivered over for condign punishment to his feudal lord, the very daimio against whom he had complained! By him, Sogoro and his wife were put to death on the cross, and their three children decapitated. It must be remembered that crucifixion here was not the lingering torment of the Roman punishment; the victim appears to have been simply bound upon the cross, uplifted before the multitude, and in that position put to death by the thrust of a spear.

Horrible? Beyond question. Japanese or Buddhist civilization must bear the reproach of this barbarity in the year 1644. And yet we must not forget that half a century afterwards, Christian England saw Elizabeth Gaunt burnt at the stake in London, for no crime but the sheltering of a refugee; that more than a hundred years later, the most Christian King of France, with all his court of lords and ladies, listened to the shrieks of Damien as the melted lead was poured into living flesh; that forty years after Sogoro's death, Giles Corey was crushed to death in Puritan America, for refusing to plead to the charge of witchcraft; and Jews, then unborn, were to perish in the flames in Catholic Spain,[1] for clinging to their ancient faith.

But humanity everywhere reveres self-sacrifice, above all, when it culminates in death. It cannot undo the wrong nor restore the dead; but of the martyr she will make a hero; the Church may make him a saint; the people shall perhaps make him a demi-god. Everywhere there is the same impulse of recognition. In Japan, the story of Sogoro became the theme of the drama, the subject of poetry and romance. To the tragic story I have told, imagination added new and weird elements. Some near the cross of the dying man thought that they heard him threaten to come back after death to the castle of his tyrant; and not long after it began to be whispered that the threat was no idle one, that his spirit had indeed returned. It is only certain that Sogoro accepted with prevision the martyrdom which came to him, dying to make others free. We cannot wonder, therefore, that his memory was cherished and revered. In course of time he was taken into the Buddhist pantheon, and he is to-day worshipped as a demi-god throughout Japan.

The monument which marks the place of martyrdom

---

[1] In the correspondence of Spinoza (Letter 74), he relates an incident which illustrates what was going on in Europe this very same year. On July 25, 1644, a Spanish nobleman was burnt at the stake for having adopted the Jewish faith, through the study of Hebrew. In the midst of the flames, when he was thought to be dead, he lifted up his voice to sing the hymn, "Unto Thee, O God, do I offer up my soul."

is of plain stone, a short obelisk set upon square foundations, the front covered with an inscription in Chinese characters. It stands outside the town near the roadside, close by a grove which formerly shadowed the castle of the daimio. On either side of it, two lofty trees unite their branches far above. Here the pious pilgrim journeys to murmur a prayer, to burn incense, to lay offerings of flowers, to invoke the intercession of the saint, or perhaps to spend the night under the gracious influences of the shrine. I almost stumbled upon one old man who was sleeping on a bed of leaves behind the monument itself.

Matoï was now requested to turn about and start for Tokio. Nothing, however, would induce him to go faster than a walk; I had forgotten to put it in the bond! He knew that his expenses were all paid by me; and that he was hired by the day. In truth, I cannot blame him for not being disposed to hurry, and thus shorten the period of so pleasant an engagement. Sometimes he seems filled with all the importance of a peripatetic Barnum, with a rare living curiosity which he is transporting about the country. At booths by the wayside, and tea-houses where I had no wish to stop, he insists on resting, and having a bite, or a cup of *saké*, at my expense, of course. Occasionally he purchases a melon, washes it most carefully at the well, peels it with dexterity, and then offers it to me, a crowd breathlessly looking on to see how it will be eaten.

Sakura.

About six o'clock we reached Funabashi, celebrated in local history as the rendezvous of the village chiefs who met here with Sogoro to frame their fatal petition to the Tycoon. The hotel was much better than the one of yesterday. At first some difficulty seemed likely to happen in regard to my passport, which, strictly speaking, does not permit me to come this way at all. Last night the landlord contented himself with a mere glance at the document, but the present innkeeper was more cautious. He read the passport slowly and carefully. It permits me to go to Nikko and over the Naka-sen-do to Kioto; but this route is in the opposite direction. The landlord came to my room soon after I entered the house, dropped on his knees, touched his forehead to the floor, and begged me to vouchsafe an explanation. There was none to give. Matoi could explain nothing. However, it was evident that although beyond treaty limits, we were making our way back to the city; and he probably concluded to let us alone.

My room is the best guest-chamber, and one of three at the rear of the house. It overlooks a little garden, or rather a sort of miniature landscape. There is an artificial island of rockwork, in a lake bordered by pigmy trees and shrubs; while a statue of Buddha graces one corner of the yard. The front of the inn is given over to the kitchen, the bath-room, and the apartments for the landlord and servants. All the rooms seem somehow to connect with one another; and every one goes about barefoot, or at least in stockings, when once the ground is left and the clean matting of the floor is touched by feet.

The maid-servants seem particularly curious; I should almost think they had never before seen a foreigner. Soon after taking possession of my room, a girl entered without knocking, dropped on her knees, touched her head to the floor, and then sat down in one corner, doubling her feet somewhere out of the way, in the usual incomprehensible fashion of the country. Fortunately I had just concluded some changes of attire; but this sort of abrupt and unannounced visits must be occasionally embarrassing. Somewhat later appeared two other maids bearing the supper-tray and the rice-buckets, and all three assisted at the evening meal. We attempted to talk a little. O-kami, the oldest, said she was eighteen; O-bata was sixteen; and O-mi-i was thirteen. There was a brief dispute who should open the eggs and who should fan his eminence the traveller. Everything he did seemed to be regarded with a kind of wonder and awe, as if he were a celestial visitor who had touched the earth for a day, but would fly away to-morrow. The loaf of bread excited the utmost curiosity. None of them appeared ever to have tasted it before, and it was interesting to watch their faces as they made the experiment at my invitation. The verdict was on the whole favourable, although O-kami appeared to think that it needed flavour, and sprinkled her share with salt, a procedure which greatly improved it, judging by her gestures and smiles. I wish I had brought with me some simple curiosities for young people. Having nothing better, I gave each of them a pin. For some moments they puzzled over its purpose and use, till O-bata thought she solved the problem by sticking it in her hair!

July 23.—My second experience of Japanese inns has been decidedly better than the first. It was quiet at an earlier hour, and I made my charioteer comprehend that he must sleep where his midnight feasts and smoking vigils would not keep me awake. The couch on the floor still seems a trifle hard, but some thirty millions of people in this country have no better, and find life worth living nevertheless. The morning was glorious; we had a good start; and a little before noon, Matoi drew up in front of the Sei-yo-ken hotel with a grand burst of speed, smiling as if he had been travelling at that pace throughout the whole journey.

CHAPTER V.

A PILGRIMAGE TO NIKKO.

Excursion with a guide—The flea-bag—The Mikado's soldiers—A Buddhist subscription-list—Telegraphs and idols—Oyama silk-weaving—A girl at the loom—Wonders of an opera-glass—The great avenue of trees—Arrival at Nikko.

July 29.—Travel without a guide not being entirely satisfactory, I am making another trip with an escort— a journey to the shrines of Nikko, nearly a hundred miles distant. It has not been at all difficult to obtain an English-speaking servant; in fact, several offered to go at merely nominal wages, for the privilege of settling all my accounts. One young man in European dress admitted that he had no experience as a valet, but he would be willing to accompany me as an interpreter. Happening to refer to my curiosity about rites and ceremonies of the Buddhist religion, he frankly informed me that he knew nothing about them whatever; he really had "no interest whatever in that kind of nonsense." But that "nonsense" may be interesting to others, if not to him. I finally selected a modest youth, Waku by name, well recommended as honest and reliable, and engaged him on trial for a week.

To begin with, he made several wise suggestions. First was the sleeping-bag, or, as I call it, the "flea-bag." Japanese beds not being furnished with sheets, the traveller of course takes his own. But sheets, as I have already found, are no protection against one of the greatest enemies of sleep in this country—the wicked flea. Persian powder and camphor only seem to excite his eagerness for blood. The flea-bag is somewhat of a defence. It consists of two sheets, sewn together in form of a huge sack, with gathering strings at the top. Two sleeves, the length of the arms, but closed, afford some slight facility for the use of the hands. When ready for sleep, you crawl like a worm into your chrysalis, tie the puckering strings about your neck, and there you are! To get inside, the flea must find your neck. Why do they hesitate to approach the face? Does the breath frighten them? Still, hunger is stronger than fear, sometimes, and the demoniacal intelligence of this insect rises occasionally superior to all human efforts to keep him from his prey.

My luggage has been compressed in small compass. Discarding all leather portmanteaus or bags, I put everything in two Japanese travelling-baskets of wickerwork, called yanagi-gori, very light, and made upon a pattern common in this country, whereby capacity may be almost doubled at the pleasure of the voyager. The cover is an exact duplicate of the basket itself, only one size larger. In way of provisions, this time I have taken more than needful. The great secret of comfortable travel in Japan seems to be to hit the happy mean, if you can, taking neither a lot of things which are only burdensome, nor omitting necessities. Tastes differ so greatly, especially in the way of food, that what is indispensable to one traveller may be omitted without the least inconvenience by another. Tinned milk, jams and marmalades, bacon, sugar, coffee, Worcestershire sauce, chow-chow, pickles, Chicago canned meats, loaves of bread, are all put down by some writers as indispensable, and all of them I have with me. Liebig's extract of beef is necessary; I find it for sale in Tokio at nearly half the Yokohama price. Then a good blanket was recommended as a great comfort and really indispensable.

At six o'clock in the morning, with three jinrikishas, one being for the luggage, our caravan started for Nikko. The morning's ride was over a flat and uninteresting country. Now and then a stout naked peasant is seen in the fields, treading the wheel which lifts the water from canals into his rice patch, just as one sees the fellah working by the banks of the Nile. What an interesting experiment it would be to take common labouring men of one country to another, and hear their

A Pilgrimage to Nikko. 41

comments! How I should like to bring an Egyptian village to Japan, or start a Japanese colony in Southern Italy or Spain, or introduce to some desert tribe of Bedouin Arabs a dozen or two Sioux from the plains of Colorado and Texas!

Many detachments of soldiers are met, all in European uniform, and engaged apparently in superintending preparations for a journey of the Mikado next month. Labourers were clearing up the paths, removing weeds and grass from the roadside up to a certain line. The people, like those of other nations, are greatly attracted by the appearance of bright uniforms and implements of war. In one cottage I counted thirteen persons, more or less undressed, all in eager expectation, waiting to see the soldiers pass. At Nakata a bridge of boats had been thrown across the river by an engineer corps for use by the Mikado; but of course, though quite complete, we were not allowed to go over it. Tired with my thirty-six miles' ride, I decided to put up at Nakata, where, at the house of the *hon-jin*, or headman, I was accommodated with comfortable quarters. Waku transformed himself into a cook, and proceeded to serve me with a variety of concoctions, palatable enough after a long day's journey, but smacking, I thought, rather more of Japanese than European cooking.

July 30.—This second day's journey has been of more interest. In village after village preparations for the welcome of the Mikado are in progress. Here and there at temples, which it may be hoped he will honour with a visit, new sentry-boxes are being set up for the imperial guards. Sometimes rich and quaint old carvings from inner shrines are taken down and affixed to flag-staffs on either side of the path; the Son of Heaven may at least honour them with a glance. One village was the proud possessor of a new temple, built evidently near the site of one destroyed by fire; and very brave it looked in its bright carvings and new paper windows. By the roadside in front was an immense sign-board, fifteen feet long by ten feet high, nearly covered with wooden slabs inscribed with Chinese characters.

"Waku, wait a minute," I cried; "what does this sign say?"

"It tell that old temple burned down, and many people give something to build new one. Those their names."

"Well, does it say how much they give?"

"All give different; some one yen, some two yen, some more. Names who give most at top; names who give little at bottom. Some give ten yen," he added, as he scanned the few names of liberal donors who headed the list. It seemed ridiculous at first. Tokagato gives ten shillings toward the new temple, and sees his munificence blazoned to the world on a shingle by the roadside! But, after all, human nature is much the same. Who shall measure the gratification of the London alderman at the publication of his name in *The Times* in response to an appeal from the Mansion House?

The newest sign of civilization may touch the symbols of the oldest religions. Telegraph-poles are planted, not by the roadside, as with us, but in the peasants' fields, particularly when a saving of distance can be accomplished. Near them I often see stone images of Buddha, to whose care the guileless peasant commits his seed, and ascribes a good crop; just as in some parts of Italy a cross is set up in a wheat-field, with results quite as certain and satisfactory. At Oyama, the whole village seems given up to the silk industry. Every house appears to have its collection of silkworms feeding on mulberry leaves, or tossing aimlessly about on their layers of clean straw. There is, too, in every cottage a corner for the silk-loom, worked by hand, where back and forth the shuttle flies through the web. It was pleasant to walk through the town and take the peasants unawares at their work. In one cottage I came upon a young girl thus weaving at the loom. The day was warm, and, in that sweet innocence of wrong-doing that pervaded Eden before the serpent entered it, she had thrown off the upper part of her gown, and sat nude to the waist, beautiful as Hebe, singing at her task. In a tiny cage above her head was a kind of cricket, which from time to time chirped an accompaniment to her song. The picture lasted but a moment or two; a step sounded; a glance at the silent and bearded barbarian standing outside, and the nymph had vanished.

I find my opera-glass a source of unfailing amusement and of infinite wonder on the part of these simple villagers. When we stop at a tea-house to rest, I prefer wandering through the town. At Mibu, a troop of children of all sizes came clattering down the road after me. Taking out my opera-glass, I looked at them, and they scattered from before it like a flock of sheep; evidently they imagined it might go off like a gun. An old woman coming near, I beckoned her, and made signs that she take a look through the instrument, whereat great and emphatic were the exclamations of wonder and amazement. That brought up a neighbour, whose delight at seeing distance abolished was equally demonstrative. Two white-robed pilgrims returning from Nikko, respectfully solicit the privilege of looking through this wonder-working glass; and the effect obtained by reversing the instrument, making near objects distant, seems to be regarded as even more marvellous than the legitimate use of it. Then a carpenter stopped planing his board, and joined the gathering crowd; a smith left his forge; the children recovered courage and increased in numbers, till I think I had the whole village peeping by turn at the distant hills or nearer objects through my glass. As we rode away, their voices united in one great shout of parting good-will, "Sa-yo-na-ra! sa-yo-na-ra!"

A drizzling rain began to make travel difficult, and I was not loth to abridge the day's journey. Put up at a poor village, Niregi, where the noise of dogs fighting in the street kept me awake half the night.

July 31.—From this point on to Nikko the road is one grand avenue between magnificent trees, whose continuity of shade was only broken by intervening villages. I never saw a road like it anywhere. If one can imagine the fine old trees of Bushy Park planted on either side of a road from London to Canterbury, set closely together, sometimes not six feet apart, he may form a conception of this royal road. As we drew nearer Nikko, we found them planted on each side of the way in double rows, so that foot-passengers walked under shade on either side of the main road. In truth, it continually suggested the long nave and aisles of some grand Gothic cathedral, like that of Seville, for instance, and crowded with worshippers; the great distinction being the indefinite length; for overhead, the branches, arched together, make even at midday a "dim religious light." For centuries the ruler of Japan was accustomed to visit Nikko either in person or by an envoy, to worship at the graves of his ancestors; and these trees were planted to shield the royal pilgrim from the sun or rain. The largest ones are nearest the holy place, and were the first planted. Near Imiachi, five miles out of Nikko, the traveller in the middle of the road looking, say forty feet ahead, cannot discern a single interstice between the line of tree trunks; it is one unbroken row of pillars, one continuous aisle. I have as yet seen nothing in Japan more grand than this avenue of trees which for more than thirty miles lines the way to the shrines of Nikko.

Pilgrims now are met with increasing frequency, returning from a visit to the holy places. In an hour I counted two hundred journeying singly or in small parties, and of every age, from the youth of a dozen years to the decrepit old man just able to hobble along. They are dressed in white, the symbol of pilgrimage in this country, as once the cockle-shell and staff were for our ancestors. Excepting a very few, every one is afoot. About two o'clock the village of Nikko was reached, and, proceeding through the long street, we found lodgment at Suzuki's hotel.

CHAPTER VI.

NIKKO AND ITS SHRINES.

Temple architecture compared—Mausoleums and shrines—The Buddhist saint—The Assisi of Japan—Tomb of Iye-yasu—Pilgrim devotions—Nikko's ruins—Statues of Amida—Waku's desecration—Return journey—"Foreign accommodation"—Arrival at Tokio.

August 1.—The traveller who comes to Nikko expecting to find magnificent temples or the full splendour of a gorgeous ritual will be disappointed. The style of temple architecture in Japan is neither grand nor beautiful, at least to Western eyes. Some of them appear positively ugly. They are generally painted vermilion, a colour which does not lend itself to religious uses, in buildings at least. The interiors seemed to me in fairly good taste, taking their object into account. There is a vast amount of interior decoration in way of wood carvings; some good, most of them indifferent, but always either gilded or painted. If a Buddhist temple can be called splendid, it is certainly a splendour peculiar to itself, and denoting rather the taste of a people and of a period than a universal ideal.

It would almost seem that everything in architecture or art which, surviving the evanescent fancy of a generation, commands universal homage, must be imbued with severe simplicity. The Greek costume, for instance, is as beautiful to-day as two thousand years ago; but by the utmost stretch of imagination, we cannot picture the fashion-plates of our time regarded with admiration half a century hence. In architecture the pyramid outlasts the tomb of the Cæsars; the Doric is grander than the Corinthian. The genius of Michael Angelo could not make St. Peter's equal in beauty to the chief temples of Gothic art, whose very builders are unknown. The shrines of India are monstrosities only because the Hindu tried, by multiplying decoration, to increase their beauty; the Mahometan conquerors succeeded because they made nearly all adornment a sin. Between the temple of Neptune at Pæstum and the most gorgeous sanctuary in Japan, there is a gulf immeasurable. One type has endured for more than twenty centuries, and its crumbling ruin commands speechless admiration to-day. The other type followed the Hindu and the Chinese in complexity of attempted adornment, and the failure is only the more complete where the ambition to succeed has been most painfully evident.

But if the temples of Nikko lack beauty, there is

TEMPLE AT NIKKO.

certainly nothing wanting of the charms of natural scenery or the interest of historic and traditionary association. Here are the tombs of Japan's greatest statesmen, and the shrines of her saints. Among these hills, from the earliest recorded period, was a Shin-to shrine. In the year A.D. 767, the first Buddhist temple was erected here by the holy man, Sho-do Sho-nin. In reading the story of his life, we almost seem to be perusing the Acta Sanctorum, so similar in many respects was the Japanese hermit to the earlier Christian saints who sought a closer communion with God in the heart of the desert. The same legends are related concerning his birth, the same portents of his coming glory; religion but repeats that story to the farther East which she had before whispered to India and Palestine.

He was born, the Japanese annals tell us, in the year A.D. 735; the answer to prayer of parents who long besought the goddess of mercy for the gift of offspring. "Various wonders accompanied his birth; a miraculous cloud hung about the cottage; flowers fell from heaven into the courtyard; a strange perfume filled the air." It is needless to say that he grew up a wonderful child, fond of prayer, different in tastes and occupation from the children of his own age. At his twentieth year he left his father's house to begin a life of solitude, contemplation, and worship; and here among these hills of Nikko he spent the greater part of his gentle life in the repetition of prayers, in the performance of penance, in

Nikko and its Shrines.

the contemplation of life's mysteries, in communion with God. Here he founded the monastery of Mangwan-ji, and here, at the ripe age of eighty-two, he passed away. Nikko is the Assisi of Japan.

With Waku I have spent a day in wandering among its holy places. A rapid mountain stream rushing through a narrow gorge divides the region of shrines and temples from that of inns and shops. Two bridges, almost side by side, span the torrent, but only one is for public use. The other, painted a bright red, looks almost as new as if finished yesterday, yet it was built in 1638, two and a half centuries ago, at the point where tradition asserts that the saint whose memory is identified with this wilderness into which he was first to penetrate, was miraculously assisted to cross the chasm. Inasmuch as nobody ever crosses that bridge nowadays, unless it be the emperor, it is not so very wonderful that no repairs of consequence have been needed for the two centuries and more it has stood there. It looks, indeed, as if it might last a dozen centuries longer, so perfect is its construction.

. The chief attraction of Nikko is the mausoleum of Iye-yasu, the Cromwell of Japan, and the founder of that dynasty which, by its policy of seclusion, gave to this country the blessing of internal and external peace for more than two centuries. Peace, it is said, may be too dearly purchased. But here, at least, it was "peace with honour," and the price was simply isolation from

Western civilization. When I think of the bloody annals of European history between 1600 and 1853; of the thousands who perished at the stake, of the millions who died on battle-fields, or of wounds and disease in camps; of the sufferings of sieges, the sack of cities, the story of man's inhumanity to man—in England, France, Spain, Germany, Ireland—I am disposed to think that the blessings of absolute peace were not too dearly purchased by Japan, by that national isolation which Iye-yasu completed, if he did not inaugurate. What could Europe have given this country that she did not have? What lessons in the practice of Christian virtues could the despotisms of the seventeenth and eighteenth centuries have taught Japan? No. She was wise to shut her gates. They were opened at a better hour.

And here at Nikko sleeps the great statesman of Japan. Through groves and courts and temples, up flights of stone steps, by carven gates and cloisters, one penetrates, till at last the hill-top and mausoleum is reached. The monument is a single bronze casting, severely simple. All about it are lofty trees; far below, through their foliage, one catches an occasional gleam from the temple roofs. It is a singularly impressive tomb. Here in the heart of a forest, in a sacred wilderness, sleeps a conqueror of whom Napoleon never heard; yet a greater than Napoleon, if greatness be measured by ultimate success. Here the weary pilgrim who has climbed the mossy steps bows his head with a reverence unfelt at Mount Vernon, in St. Paul's, or by the Seine; for he is standing not merely by the sepulchre of a soldier, but by the shrine of a demi-god. Even Waku, who is neither Buddhist nor Shinto nor Christian, deemed it the part of prudence not to carry his infidelity too far, and knelt in reverent obeisance.

It is remarkable how well the Japanese do everything they attempt in bronze or stone when compared with their wooden architecture. The stone steps leading to the tomb just visited are beautiful specimens of masonry, and the walls of castles, the embankments of rivers, show what they might have accomplished. Near one temple just visited there is a stone cistern for holy water, the "On-Chodzu-Ya," made of a single block of polished granite about nine feet long, and perhaps four feet high. So accurately is it poised that water conducted into it gently overflows on every side in exactly equal volumes. As we approached, a number of pilgrims were performing their ablutions in an anxious and eager manner that certainly indicated no lack of faith in its virtue. An old man in attendance poured the water upon their hands; they washed the dust from their feet in a stone trough at the foot of the cistern, and a few even rinsed their mouths, as if conscious that much sin adhered thereto, which no doubt it did. What unnumbered millions may here have sought to cleanse themselves from sin, since this font was here set up in 1618—two years before that first Puritan emigration to New England, which laid the foundations of the American Commonwealth.

It is useless to attempt the description of the various tombs, shrines, and temples at Nikko; they are different and yet similar, like the churches of Rome or the temples of Egypt. Of more interest to me than the carvings of the temples were the lofty trees which surrounded them, looking as if they had been waving their branches for a thousand years. Some of them I should think were almost two hundred feet in height. I measured one, and at two feet above the ground found a circumference of over twenty feet. In many places the trees are enclosed and revered as sacred, usually because the site of some act of a saint or the apparition of a goddess.

It is a tiresome thing—this sight-seeing. A few hours is enough. Yesterday, leaving behind the great temples and shrines, we followed the banks of the Daiya-gawa, passing through a suburb of Nikko quite distinct from the pilgrim's part of the town. The streets are all at right angles, and through many of them runs a sparkling stream of pure water in pebble-lined aqueducts. Everywhere between this and the pilgrim town are evidences that at one time Nikko was of far greater importance and magnificence than to-day. Street after street along the hillside is lined with solid walls of massive masonry, sometimes six to eight feet high, and from three to five feet thick at the top. Flights of stone steps lead upward into spaces of desolation choked

Nikko and its Shrines.

with brambles, covered with thickets. Here and there one finds a paved court thus enclosed; but empty, desolate; and each of these, Waku tells me, was the site of some temple or monastery of ancient days which has disappeared, leaving only the stone foundations.

A mile or so beyond this part, the scenery becomes wilder and more romantic. The stream is now a series of rapids forced by precipitous contracting rocks into narrow channels, at one point barely six feet wide. A turn in the winding road suddenly reveals a long row of stone statues of Amida Buddha, seated side by side facing the river in a grand semicircle. Guide-books and different travellers have put the number at several hundreds; but though I counted twice, I could not make them number above a hundred and forty. It is said that some years ago the largest of these stone statues was washed down the river by a flood, arriving at Imaichi, six miles distant, in perfect safety! When one looks at the statue, and then at the rocky bed of the stream, his faith will be stronger than mine to credit this statement, even though it is given as a fact without qualification by good authority. As little Paul Dombey remarks about the tale of the wild bull and the boy who asked too many questions, "I don't believe *that* story."

At this point the scenery is particularly beautiful. Far in the distance rises the peak of the sacred mountain Nan-tai-Zan, then come the lesser hills, with thick forests intervening; directly in front is the dashing tumbling torrent, while at the left, with half-closed eyes and folded hands, sit in eternal contemplation the statues of Amida. It is the perfection of quietude. Yet it was not always as to-day. The path which winds by the side of the torrent ends in a thicket; but far within its shadowy depths, overgrown by moss and tangled weeds, one can see the continuation of the heavy masonry which formed the ancient wall along the road. At one place stone steps lead from the path down to the very edge of the torrent.

Most of these statues are about life-size; many are headless, and otherwise bear evidence of no reverent treatment. A few carry their heads in their laps! Still it is not entirely deserted by pilgrims, for the printed prayers on slips of paper affixed to the stone images, and coins left in their laps, show that now and then some of reverent tendencies still visit this ancient shrine.

I caught Waku pilfering the coins from the laps of the images, and remonstrated with him. "It is much better to give them to children than to leave them out here," replied the practical youth. I hope he reconciled his proceeding to his conscience, for he gathered into his sleeves every loose "cash" he could find. He is a type of young Japan, half sceptical of all religions, and yet not absolutely without reverence. I have met in Continental Europe young men who ridiculed the faith of their fathers, but who nevertheless took pains to cross themselves on entering a church or cathedral. So with

Waku. He is not a Christian by any means, nor will he confess to the least leaning toward the faith of his ancestors. Yet he washed face and hands at the holy font, and when he thinks I am not noticing, I hear him rubbing his palms before a shrine. He tells me that under the old government of Tycoons these images were well cared for, but that since the accession of the Mikado they have been permitted to take care of themselves.

August 5.—Before going over the Naka-sen-do, I had planned to return to Tokio; otherwise it would have been more convenient perhaps to have taken Nikko as a part of the journey. Early one morning we set out for return to the capital. As the way was downhill, Waku suggested that a third vehicle simply for our baskets was really superfluous, as indeed it was; for, though each jinrikisha was drawn by a single coolie, we covered forty-five miles before reaching Temmo, where we put up for the night.

The village is insignificant, but the accommodation very fair. After being shown into the guest-chamber, a servant appeared, bearing a rude unpainted pine table, which was carefully deposited in the centre of the room. Next came a rickety article intended to pass for a foreign chair, and then the little maid-servants gathered, expecting to see me make myself " comfortable " by sitting bolt upright in the middle of the empty room, after riding all day! An extra charge was inserted in the account for "foreign accommodation."

The next day another early start; indeed, it is impossible to do otherwise in this country. You must get up when the household begins to awaken to the day's duties; a quiet morning nap is out of the question. Our men struck across the country from one main road to another, on a path barely wide enough for a single karuma; but the coolies jog merrily on, naturally preferring their hard work to come in the cool of the day. I do not see many birds in this country; but nature is animated enough in other ways. Never elsewhere during much travel in many lands have I seen spiders so numerous or of so many species. While the morning dew is yet clinging to their webs, they seem to be everywhere in myriads, and of greater size than one finds elsewhere as a rule. Streams ten feet wide I have again and again seen spanned by their tiny cables.

At one point in our pathway a small frog leaped from an adjoining thicket, holding in his mouth a huge dragon-fly almost as large as himself. He had somehow caught it by the head, and though making for his element, was impeded and disconcerted by the terrible buzzing kept up by his victim. Holding my umbrella before him, he was easily taken. There was no use in depriving him of his breakfast, which he had certainly caught with skill, and on being released he sprang at once into the stream, still holding fast to the head of his victim.

About the middle of the afternoon we struck into the

great highway leading to Tokio, and henceforth our route was even and well-travelled. Overnight we put up at Oyami, in one of the best of Japanese inns, and the next morning, without further incident, we arrived at the Sei-yo-ken.

CHAPTER VII.

PLANS AND PREPARATIONS.

The route decided — The mountain road — Decision to go alone — Disadvantages of being "personally conducted" — The "squeezing" process universal — Note for future excursionists.

Tokio, August 6.—My plan for the long journey is settled. I shall try to do the Naka-sen-do, or mountain highway, leading from the eastern to the western capital, through the heart of Japan.

I have decided also to go entirely alone without courier or guide of any sort. European residents here tell me the plan will be likely to involve me in all sorts of difficulties, particularly from my almost total ignorance of the language. Missionaries, of course, are constantly making trips and excursions in various directions; but they say that nobody with any regard for comfort would attempt it, unless he could speak Japanese. In case of sickness or accident it might be very unpleasant. But, then, I must take care not to be sick, nor to have accidents.

There is much to be said in favour of it. My Japanese

Plans and Preparations. 61

friends in Tokio, while advising against it, tell me it is entirely practicable; that I run no danger of insult or robbery. . Then, too, my trip to Nikko and back taught me some of the disadvantages of being " personally conducted." Waku spoke English fairly well; he was a good cook and valet, and as honest a boy as any traveller could expect to find for the wages. Nevertheless, he was no help in directions where I most wanted assistance. Of differences between the Buddhist sects of Japan, or even between Buddhism and the State religion or Sintooism, he seemed to know nothing, and to care nothing. Perhaps he knew as much in regard to such matters as most people of his class. A Japanese traveller in England, who should seek to learn from an English servant the distinctions between Methodists and Presbyterians, might get no clearer answers than Waku gave me. But it was with difficulty he could be induced even to ask information in regard to the simplest affairs. On the journey to Nikko I saw an old man apparently fishing in his half-submerged rice-field. The improbability of its being a good place for angling excited my curiosity. I stopped the jinrikisha.

"Waku, what is that man trying to catch?"

"I do not know, sir."

"Do the jinrikisha-men know?"

He asked them. They professed entire ignorance. Meantime the old fisherman at a few rods' distance kept scooping up something or other.

"Waku, ask the fisherman what he is catching out there in the rice-field?"

But this he was decidedly reluctant to do. It was only by my calling to the half-frightened fisherman, and attempting in broken jargon to put the questions myself, that Waku interposed and obtained the information. The old peasant was dipping up in his net little eels about the size of one's finger, out of which, I learned later, the Japanese make a sort of broth.

By far the greatest objection to him was the fact that he stood between me and the people I wished to study. It seemed absolutely impossible to make him comprehend that I preferred what appeared to him annoyance, rather than the seclusion he attempted to procure for me. We arrived, for instance, at an inn, and were welcomed with profuse hospitality. After a few minutes' conversation with the landlord, I was usually conducted to the best room. Thenceforth I was like the "Man in the Iron Mask," a prisoner of State, of whom he was head-gaoler. No native servant was ever permitted to serve me; he alone cooked my food, served it, answered all calls, was ready to help me in every way I didn't care for, and to save me from every attempt to make myself understood. If I wished to buy anything, he completed the bargain, and at a price inevitably higher than I had to pay when strolling about Tokio alone. I don't think he suggested always the greater price, but "squeezing" is so invariably the custom that it was recognized that he might come back for his commission. In China, India, Egypt, Spain, France, Italy (to speak merely of my own experience), and, I suppose, everywhere else, the traveller who bargains through an interpreter must always pay more than he need pay alone.

In short, if I had come to Japan to journey at my ease, I could hardly have a better servant. But I want to "rough it" a little. It annoys me to be kept away from the people, or to have them driven away from me. By travelling alone, independent of servant or guide, I may have some vexations and annoyances, but the compensations, I think, will more than repay.

The food question is solved. Experience on two journeys has taught me that one may very easily cumber himself with too many "indispensable" articles of food. Every one's taste in this respect is different; but when a traveller is disposed to do with little, he can get on with nothing European but Liebig's extract of meat. Half a dozen little pots will serve a single traveller for a month, I am told; and, although it probably contains little nutritive substance, it provides a flavour that is most relishable. Stir a small spoonful, or even less, in a bowl of hot water, with a little salt and cayenne pepper, and with boiled rice to suit, you have a soup fit for a prince—a hungry prince, of course.

The distance between Tokio and Kioto, over the mountain road, is 335 miles. I propose to take about three weeks for the trip. A small pocket-dictionary, giving Japanese equivalents for English words is the basis of all possible inter-communication. A Japanese friend has written out for me, in Chinese characters, a few phrases, more especially for use in emergencies.[1] I have the Japanese phrase, "I want," at my tongue's end. Then it shall go hard with me if I do not find a Japanese substantive to follow after. But supposing the Japanese wish something of me? That sort of difficulty is not likely to find easy solution.

The Naka-sen-do has been a royal road for a thousand years. The first part is rather uninteresting. For this reason I go to Honjo, about fifty miles distant, in a stage-coach, which leaves this evening before midnight. The manager of the hotel has bought my ticket, and one of the Japanese servants will accompany me to the booking-office from which it starts. He will explain that I am to be set down at Honjo to-morrow morning, and directed to a certain inn; and then, I suppose, the fun of this sort of travel will begin. I have sent all my heavy luggage by steamer to Kobe, and am very tired after a long day of preparation.

[1] His style, however, was so purely classical that I found no innkeeper who could read them. Fortunately they were not absolutely required.

CHAPTER VIII.

OVERLAND TOWARD KIOTO.

A midnight start—Inquisitive fellow-passengers—Honjo—Stroll about the town—Prevalence of blindness—School children—The silk industry—Japanese bargains—Village industries—Crossing the Umezawa Pass—Arrival at Ozawa.

August 7.—It seemed to me that I had but just dropped asleep when the servant knocked at the door with the announcement that everything was in readiness; and that the man I had engaged to take me to the stage-office was waiting at the door. A few minutes later we were passing swiftly through the streets of Tokio. Nearly all the shops were closed; only a few dealers in *bric-à-brac* were displaying their wares on the pavement. Not a sound of noisy revelry to be heard, not a drunken man to be seen. How different will be the streets of London, Paris, or New York, a few hours later this Saturday night! But this is a heathen country, barbarous, uncivilized. ??

Few people, I am afraid, would consider my plan very wise. And, indeed, set down at midnight at a Japanese hostelry, amid a crowd of curious passengers— mine the only European face—utterly unable to say a single sentence correctly, it *was* productive of a feeling of loneliness. Every new passenger looked at me, and then took occasion to question the proprietor of the coach, gaining little satisfaction evidently. Presently the passengers began to climb into the coach to secure their places. I followed their example, taking a front seat with the driver. Two lean, half-starved-looking little ponies were led forward, and with no little difficulty hitched or tied to the vehicle. The horses here are only half-broken, and that badly; but they work with a will, when once induced sufficiently. Two coaches were filled with passengers, and just at the hour of midnight the ostler let go the horses' heads, and we were off at full speed. Past the temple of Confucius, now a library; past the splendid grove of Hongo; over the bridge on which Sogoro presented his petition to the shogun, two hundred and fifty years ago, and was crucified for his audacity; through narrow streets and lanes, we dashed at a most uncomfortable rate toward the great imperial road. It was strange to be thus commencing a day, when everything was closed or closing up. It was nearly an hour before we had fairly turned out of Tokio, and were striking across the country on the Naka-sen-do.

Overland toward Kioto.

The novelty of the scene at first prevented desire of sleep, but toward morning I found it very difficult to keep awake, and yet was obliged to hold fast to prevent being pitched headlong under the horses' heels. Their speed was something marvellous. They were not permitted to slacken pace; it was a break-neck gallop up hill and down; and the way they turned round corners at full speed would have elicited praise even from an old Californian stage-driver. Every six or eight miles we changed horses; and the panting of the poor beasts showed the exertions they had put forth. At these stations tea was handed in little cups to the passengers, who repaid by a gratuity. The air was neither cold nor sultry, and it was easy to see why passengers preferred to travel by night, when comfort is the main object. At one point the coach stopped, and all the passengers alighted, apparently without reason—disappearing down the road. It seemed most unlikely that they had reached their journey's end, so I followed their example, and found the road to be very bad and steep for a short distance.

At the first glimpse of dawn, the country-people began to bestir themselves. Smoke was seen issuing from the cottages, denoting preparations for the morning meal. It was curious to observe the difference between town and country in this respect. We passed houses of peasants, where before sunrise every one was up, some at work in the granaries, or cultivating the little patches about their houses; while further on we rattled through the long straggling street of some village in which not even a dog was astir. It would seem to be a universal condition of town life everywhere to keep later hours than the rustic population.

We reached Kumagai, forty-two miles from Tokio, about seven in the morning. All the passengers here alighted and took breakfast. I preferred, however, to wait until I reached my destination, two hours further on. Here we changed coaches, and I no longer had a seat by the driver, but sat among the other passengers. Gradually they became communicative to an embarrassing extent. One of them asked me a question which I did not understand (later on I learned to know the phrase better; it was an inquiry regarding my destination). "Wakadi masen," I replied, a phrase which means both "I do not know" and "I do not understand." It seemed to have been taken in the former sense, for the phrase was repeated by one or two with laugh-provoking comments. Possibly they thought it very strange for a foreigner to be journeying into the interior without a destination in view. I produced my passport, and explained that the Naka-sen-do was in general my route, and that I was bound from Tokio to Kioto. That seemed satisfactory. One young man, therefore, searched among his luggage and found a small writing-desk, from which he produced both his business-card and a photograph of himself in European costume, which he begged me to accept, ending by inviting me to come to his house and sleep that night. It was an invitation I should like to have accepted, but my plan was to leave the Naka-sen-do at Hongo for a less-beaten road; and I should not, therefore, go through Takasaki, where he lived. I fear he did not entirely comprehend my refusal, for when we reached Hongo at ten o'clock he seemed quite surprised that I should stop there instead of going on with him.

A ride of fifty-five miles at night had made me very sleepy. A Japanese boy, to whom I entrusted my luggage, guided me to the principal inn, where good accommodation awaited me. After a breakfast of rice, fish, and chocolate, I drew together the screens of my room, and, lying down on the matted floor, did not awaken until nearly four in the afternoon.

Started out to see the town, accompanied by a servant of the inn, who of his own accord acted as my guide. It is quite a large and flourishing place of about three thousand five hundred inhabitants. All the temples are well kept and evidently well patronized; a sign everywhere of prosperity as well as piety. Hongo is one of the great silk marts of this part of Japan. Nearly every shopkeeper deals in raw silks, buying directly from the peasantry. Heavy skeins of shining yellow hang about the doors. Women from the country go from one dealer to another, displaying their skeins of silk, and endeavouring to get the highest price possible.

When a bargain is finally concluded, the dealer claps his hands noisily together: the deed is done. "Give me your hand on it," says the American, after concluding a bargain. In Japan, men do not shake hands, so they clap their hands instead. Blindness strikes me as the greatest scourge of the people. Lameness is very rare. In the three weeks I have been in the country I have not seen a hunchback or a cripple, and not a single child with that unhealthy, sickly complexion which often characterizes the dwellers in the back streets of great cities. But, on the other hand, I should think one in twenty—possibly even one in fifteen—of the persons one meets, is either partially or wholly blind. They are apparently better off than those similarly affected elsewhere; I believe they are money-lenders often by profession, and certainly I have not seen one begging. In the highway occasionally I notice them travelling by twos and threes in single file, each keeping fast hold to the one in front—" the blind leading the blind."

Returning to the inn, I concluded successfully my first bargain for a conveyance. Calling the innkeeper, I managed to convey the ideas suggested by the words, "I want—jin-rikisha." A stout, good-natured fellow soon made his appearance, and upon him I launched another question, "To-morrow morning—early—I go —to—Ichi-no-miya;—how much?" I dare say the grammatical construction was altogether wrong, but the first end of language was nevertheless attained—*he understood!* After thinking the matter over a minute, he told me a yen and a half, about three and sixpence, for a distance of twenty-two miles. I had no idea what he should charge, but presumed he was asking for more than the usual price; so, as a matter of principle, I told him that was too much—" Takai! Takai!" At this he expostulated forcibly; and I ended by engaging him, as I intended to do all the time.

August 8th.—Up early and packed, ready to start long before the rest of the house was stirring. Breakfasted on beef-tea (Liebig's) with rice, and boiled eggs. At seven the luggage was duly packed into the karuma, and I called for my account. It was such an outrageous overcharge that I somewhat fiercely protested, showing him at the same time my account at Omiya on this road, where Waku and myself were charged far less than what he presumed to charge me alone. He studied the account for a while; concluded, I hope, that one foreigner was not absolutely inexperienced in Japan travelling, and cut down his charge to about half, which I paid.[1]

About seven we were off. Soon after passing through the town, we left the Naka-sen-do, and took a cross-path just wide enough for a single vehicle. The

[1] I may add that this was the only instance, during my two months' travelling alone in Japan, in which I was unreasonably overcharged at a hotel.

mountains now began to be visible, and the scenery to improve. My jinrikisha-man was very stout, above the average of natives. He drew me and all my luggage over not the best of roads, and never once stopped for tea-house or wayside bower until he had substantially

A MORNING CALL.

completed his journey at Tomioka, over twenty miles distant. He was so good-natured, in fact, that I felt no very great indignation at his beguiling me out of the price of his dinner, which, however, I am sorry to say, he did twice the same day, and very cleverly. While

I was eating my midday luncheon at the Tomioka inn, he appeared outside, rubbing his stomach to indicate his hunger, and requesting twenty sen to buy food. This was by no means in the bond. I gave it, however, as he had served me very well. It was not until the next day, when, on finding a translator to my bill for dinner, I learned *his* dinner was also included therein !

While he was resting, I stepped out to take a stroll through the town. Just beyond the restaurant, I saw some children emerging from school, and stopped on the opposite side of the street to look at them. They came out with none of the rude boisterousness which characterizes scholars at home, but walked sedately and quietly with books and slates under their arms. The first to come out were not a little startled, evidently, at the sight of a bearded foreigner looking at them. They stopped a moment, and then, with a courtesy which I wish I could imagine possible in an English town or American village, made an exceedingly respectful bow, and passed on. Of course I returned the salutation. The next ones following repeated their civility, and then as fast as the pupils came to the front they stopped and made profound reverences all along the line. It was a very pretty picture, and quite well illustrated the polite bearing of the Japanese, who are thus trained to civility from childhood. Before a baby can speak, almost before it can totter alone, it is taught to lift the hand to the forehead on receiving a gift; and I never saw a child fail to make this signal of respect and gratitude without being reproved or reminded of the omission by some bystander.

Tomioka is another centre of the silk-growing industry, and in nearly every village through which we passed the majority of the inhabitants were thus engaged. Their primitive processes were very interesting to me. The first step, after you have cocoons, is to unwind them and make a thread. But how is this to be accomplished? A handful of cocoons is thrown into a small pot of water, simmering over a little charcoal fire. The hot water appears to unloosen the fixed end of the thread, so that when the operator dabbles about with a bit of broom she picks up half a dozen almost invisible threads which she fastens to the side of the kettle for use as wanted. Three or four of these she deftly twists into a tiny thread, and fastens it to a reel, and this, turned with the left hand, swiftly unrolls the cocoons till they end in the black and shrivelled bodies of the dead little spinners. Sometimes one cocoon gives out before the others; then a new one is made to take its place. It is curious to see the cocoons bobbing about in the hot water; indeed, no better illustration could be given of the operation than the unrolling of half a dozen small spools of thread in a bowl, the threads unwinding by the weight of their spools. How many centuries have passed since this crude method of turning a worm's shroud into a brilliant fabric was first discovered! I should like, indeed, to give some fair girl-graduate in England or America a piece of Chinese or Japanese silk and a bushel of cocoons, and test her ingenuity in devising the methods by which one becomes the other. "Make for me," I should like to say, "a yard of silk ribbon, and you shall have a thousand pounds. Here is a bit of silken stuff; there is the raw material. In ancient times, when our ancestors were dressed in skins, a people whom we now affect to despise, learned to unwind these cocoons, to twist the threads, to set up the warp and pass the shuttle, and to make a fabric which you are proud to wear. You have been taught all the secrets of philosophy, of science, of mathematics; see, now, if your culture, the best that civilization can afford, will assist you to evolve the processes by which this fabric is made!"

The simplicity of process is equalled by ingenuity of implement. The reel by which the separate filatures of the different cocoons are twisted into a single thread is exceedingly ingenious, but not easily described. I suppose the same article, duly patented in England or America, would hardly be sold for less than a guinea or so; here it costs about two shillings.

It pleases me, also, to see how generally these simple processes are carried on by the peasantry in their own homes. Let me give a glimpse of a picture whose counterpart I have seen more than once to-day. The village consists of one long and somewhat straggling street. In the rear of each dwelling is a little garden beyond which are rice-fields, and in the distance the everlasting hills, glorious and beautiful. You stop for a moment at the house of a peasant to beg a glass of water. The afternoon is warm and sultry, the screens have been taken down, you look directly through the house to the gardens beyond. The mother, perhaps, of the peasant is unwinding cocoons, the young wife is reeling the silk into skeins; her baby is sleeping on the clean mat in the best room, protected from flies and gnats by a bamboo frame covered with netting; they are happy and contented.

Suppose now we are able to afford this little community the blessings of Manchester civilization, what shall we effect? Increased happiness? I doubt it. We shall introduce the factory system in place of home labour. The young mother who now works by the side of her sleeping babe, ready to attend to every want, must then leave it to strangers at daybreak, that she may tend the machinery which will do the work of a hundred hands. Of course the outcome will be greater in the factory than in a hundred cottages—at which Capital will duly rejoice. But the mothers of these new-born children, will they be better paid? Will their lives be more elevated in tone and character? Will they be the gainers in quality and quantity of happiness? Will infant life be prolonged? Will the duties of motherhood be better performed? We have only to consult the reports of the Registrar-General and the Judicial Reports of the Home Department; or better, perhaps, to walk through the streets of a great factory town after nightfall, for replies to these questions. The waste of infant life in Manchester and other centres of industry where women are thus employed is terrible beyond expression. We have not yet solved all the problems of life with our superior civilization.

The route to Ichi-no-Miya, about three miles beyond Tomioka, was one of the prettiest imaginable, the road passing through an avenue of tall cryptomerias, and facing always the magnificent mountains. The place itself is but a small village of silk-workers, with rather more than its share of tea-houses and singing girls. My man set me down at a somewhat questionable-looking inn, took his pay, and started homeward. The place, however, was quiet, and the accommodation on the whole so fair that I concluded to go no further to-day. Visited an old Shinto temple, rather neglected in appearance, but once capable of attracting crowds of pilgrims. There is little noteworthy about the town except its situation, which is very pretty.

August 9.—A most uncomfortable night, due to the hard floor and the fleas, which were undeterred even by my usually secure defences. Added to these discomforts, I found a heavy rain pouring down, effectually preventing my getting on, as I had hoped, at once after breakfast. My resolution to remain longer in case the rain continued was with difficulty expressed. I packed everything up ready to start at any time; this was taken as a suggestion to call a jinrikisha. I succeeded, however, finally in getting this sentence into comprehensible Japanese: "Rain all day, *I stay to-night;* rain stop—I go away." The jinrikisha was sent away, and I was left to myself.

It was impossible to stay contentedly indoors, and although still drizzling, I started out with umbrella, dictionary, and opera-glass, on a tour of observation. The first house I came to was quite open to the street, and all its occupants were busily at work; two pretty girls unwinding cocoons, the mother reeling the silk into large skeins, while the father was making a kind of trap for fish or eels, a bamboo affair somewhat on the principle of the Chinese puzzle into which, when you put your fingers, they are with difficulty withdrawn. Into a long cylinder of open basket-work, a cover or trap-door is inserted in such a manner that the fish or eel finds little difficulty in pressing through to the bait, but no way of escaping. I showed them my opera-glass, eliciting the usual exclamations of delighted wonder.

Somewhat farther on, I found an old cottager busily twisting a straw rope. I almost think he made a yard a minute, of good, serviceable rope, from nothing but common straw, twisting it, or rolling it, rather, in a peculiar way between his palms. He saluted me as I entered with the uniform courtesy which belongs almost naturally to Japanese, but betrayed no further curiosity at my presence—working away at his rope, the completed part of which he kept extended by using his foot as an extra hand. I tried to imitate the process, which seemed simple enough apparently, but failed miserably. The usual crowd of lookers-on gathered about his door, and I fancied the old man seemed a little proud to have his more prosperous neighbours come to his humble cottage and salute him, merely for the purpose of gazing at the foreigner. At any rate, he quitted his work, and presently brought me out some cheap sugar confectionery and a poor little black charcoal-holder, with which to light my pipe. After some conversation, exceedingly rudimentary of course, I arose to go, when one of the neighbours touched his nose and pointed out his own dwelling, a sort of invitation to call on him. He was about sixty years old, powerfully built, with fine features, and evidently belonged to a higher class than the commonalty of the neighbourhood. Taking me into one of the rooms of his house, he showed me a lot of ancient Japanese armour and great swords hanging against the wall, all of which may once have done service. I fancy he belonged to the *samurai* or warrior caste of Japan, and that these were weapons which perhaps had been handed down from father to son for many generations.

As another curiosity he brought me a sheet of thick paste-board, covered with the eggs of the silkworm. I happened to think of a little pocket-microscope which I had picked up in Paris, technically used, I believe, for counting the number of strands in fine linen, and, taking it from my pocket, I placed it over the thickly clustered eggs, and asked him to look. To my surprise, it seemed to make him almost wild with wonder and excitement. Probably he had never before looked through any sort of magnifying glass. His neighbours were equally inexperienced, and I found this simple lens even more of a curiosity than my opera-glass.

Proceeding on through the narrow street in the misty rain, I heard a cooper at work, and went in to see him. Seated on the floor, surrounded by finished staves, he was making little buckets such as the Japanese use to carry water. First he twisted a bamboo strip into a strong hoop. Within this he set up the staves, two of them being considerably longer than the rest, and placed opposite each other as supports for the handle. As soon as the outline of the bucket was thus formed, he pounded down the hoops, deftly using his feet to turn it about, while manipulating it otherwise with his hands. The Japanese, it has long been remarked, are specially skilful in the employment of their feet in manual labour. The Hindu artisan squats upon his feet before his work, where the Japanese, seated on the ground, would employ his lower limbs to almost as great advantage as his hands. Seeing some cards containing silkworm eggs hanging from the ceiling, I indicated my wish for nearer inspection as an excuse to show him the microscopic lens, and it was really a delight to hear the excited tone in which he called to his wife within to leave her work and look through the instrument which so wonderfully magnified everything. The common people, I notice, express very much by their intonations; somewhat as a child who, wishing to indicate quantity, says "*EVER* so much!" with a curiously prolonged accentuation of the capitalized word which cannot exactly be put into print.

The rain having ceased, I went back to the inn, called for boiled rice and hot water, made out a very fair meal, and then asked for my reckoning. This is a matter for much computation, each item being written out at length in Chinese and Japanese characters. When finally brought, it was only forty sen—about an English shilling—for a residence of almost twenty-four hours. This man had evidently charged me a fair, ordinary rate, and thus afforded me a sort of standard for testing future accounts; something I could not have had if Waku had accompanied me. I paid him twenty sen extra as "tea-money," a gratuity which the host duly acknowledged by dropping on his knees and touching the floor with his forehead. Two stout fellows were waiting with their vehicles outside, and about two o'clock we set out for Ozawa.

The route passes over a steep hill, and descends into a narrow valley, through which we made slow progress owing to the condition of the roads. At Nanzai, a village about three miles from Ichi-no-miya, the road practicable for wheeled vehicles in this direction ends,

G

and further progress must be accomplished on foot or with a pack-horse. The two coolies strapped my baskets on their backs, and, making signals for me to follow, set out upon a narrow path leading by the Umezawa Pass to the village of Ozawa. At some points the way is very steep, and I found it a little difficult to keep pace with my guides, burdened as they were. The peasantry have built their houses far up the hillside; in fact, they carry on agricultural operations by means of irrigation quite to the summit of the pass. At one place, from the door of a cottage by the wayside, a child, three or four years old, came out to play, without noticing my approach until he was within six feet of where I stood. Then, with the most terrified shriek a frightened child could possibly give, he rushed towards the door, and flung himself into the startled mother's arms. Probably he had never before in his life seen a foreigner; but it is a little annoying to one's sense of the fitness of things to find himself invariably regarded by dogs with suspicion, and by children with terror!

From the summit of the pass we turned downward into a broad and pleasant valley, and came presently to the long straggling village of Ozawa, on the banks of a shallow river. The inn to which my guides conducted me was rather uninviting at first sight, but the room finally given up to me was entirely satisfactory; it was an upper chamber, with a large window overlooking the river, scarcely three rods away, and the mountains in the distance. Went out for a walk and found some ironworks under Government direction; and on calling at the office, found a young book-keeper who could speak a little English. After a short call, I invited him to come and see me at the inn, and about sundown he was ushered into my room. He learned English at the Tokio University, and of course does not speak it with much fluency. We got on, however, very well. He told me he was in Government employ at a salary of about ten yen a month (about thirty shillings in English silver), not much according to our notions, but sufficient for living in Japan, except that it permits gratification of but few tastes. He advises me to leave the valley at this point, as otherwise I should miss a very interesting shrine and a fine mountain pass, to be gained by another route. Referring to a young lady about the inn, apparently the daughter of the house, he told me that she was formerly what I believe Mr. Leckey calls a "priestess of humanity" at Ichi-no-miya; but that she was now married. After assisting me about some phrases which I wished written in Japanese, he took his departure, and I spent the evening in writing.

CHAPTER IX.

A CROSS-COUNTRY EXCURSION.

Ironworks at Ozawa—A Japanese engineer—Exploration of a mine—First ride on native pony—Mio-gi-san—Attempts at conversation—Rustic bridges—Spiders and leeches—On the Naka-sen-do—Over Usui pass—Karuizawa—Chanting pilgrims.

August 10.—While taking a stroll through the village this morning, I was addressed by a Japanese gentleman in European costume, who turned out to be a Government official just arrived from Tokio, to inspect the ironworks. He was by all odds the finest-looking Japanese I have ever seen, and one of the best educated and well informed. He has studied for nearly eight years in England, which explains his command of the language, and perhaps a choice of adjectives; everything disagreeable is "nasty"—it is "nasty weather, a nasty town," etc. As he was about to make an inspection of a mine he invited me to accompany him. After a steep climb of half a mile, we reached the opening, and, provided with lanterns and guides, we clambered down a rough passage for several hundred feet. It was the first I had visited, and so comparisons are impossible. I quite endorse his judgment, however, that it was "a nasty place." The miners are all convicted criminals; the mining department contracts for their labour at sixteen sen each a day (about fivepence) without food. My new acquaintance invited me to spend a day or two with him, but as the weather was again fine, I concluded to get on, and to reach, if possible, the shrines of Mio-gi-san before night.

My reckoning at the inn amounted as before to about an English shilling, just forty sen in fact, including some excellent brook trout which were furnished for breakfast. After dinner a pack-horse was sent for, and my baskets and travelling bags tied to the wooden saddle; then a thick blanket was placed over all, and in a most inglorious fashion I mounted the noble steed. Amid the shouts of "Sa-yo-na-ra," we started off up the hillside.

I have a secret suspicion that I should have cut but a sorry figure in that journey up the mountain-side, had any foreign eyes been looking on. Aloft, seated as it were on a tottering throne, of which the footstool was the horse's neck, awkwardly holding to the front lest the animal should rear, and behind lest it should stumble, was the traveller. With the guidance of the steed he had nothing to do; that belonged to the coolie, who led the beast by a long rope, looped at the end so that it might be thrown over his shoulder. His costume was that of a Japanese rustic; his hat was an inverted bowl, made of grass, light and comfortable under a hot sun, and his simple garment gracefully tucked up about his waist permitted perfect freedom of locomotion to the brown sinewy limbs. The horse was a rough, shaggy pony, of which I was very suspicious at first, but he acted so well on the whole that my regard for him greatly increased before the journey's end. We climbed the steepest kind of mountain paths, and descended others as abrupt as an ordinary stairway, but he never once stumbled or lost his footing. True, I could not admire his taste for walking on the narrow edge of a precipice, when the side next the mountain was equally smooth, and vastly more secure to my notion; and more than once I was compelled to shout to my guide, and request that the pony be brought back to the middle of the road. Whenever we approached a bit of path more particularly slippery or steep, the boy would call attention to it by shouting, "Hai! hai! Kore, kora!"[1] and it was curious to watch the animal at these words, prick up his ears and pick his way with especial care. With regard to his own rights, he had very definite notions; whenever on the ascent he considered it time to take a breathing spell, he stopped, and it was quite useless for his owner to pull the halter,

---

[1] "Go on" (literally "henceforth"); or perhaps "Kore! kore!"—Here! here!

or exhort him to go, until he had fairly rested; then he started on without notice, as a matter of course. Twice on the journey he was newly shod with straw shoes, of which we carried an extra pair or two.

At the summit of the pass was obtained one of the most magnificent views that I have ever seen in any country. Valley after valley, mountain range beyond mountain range, all green as in spring-time, and fading away into apparently illimitable space, combined to form a picture such as Turner might have imagined, but upon which as a reality I have never before looked. It did not resemble European scenery; it had no likeness to the Rocky Mountains, or the Adirondacks of America; but seemed to combine some beauties of each with a special charm of its own. As I saw it to-day, there were the same purple tints over the most distant hills, which make Italian landscapes so beautiful, combined with the verdure of the Westmoreland glens and the cultivation of the Swiss valleys. The air was full of chirping and singing in notes unknown, but there were no pastures; it was almost "still-life." The scene as I saw it may perhaps never have been seen by a European before, since, though the district is well known, the path is quite primitive and out of the usual routes.

We descended into the valley, and wound slowly along through village after village. I very soon had enough experience in riding, and preferred to walk somewhat in advance of my luggage. At our approach children would quit their play and scud away to the family fireside, to arouse the older members from noontime siesta, that they might not be taken unawares. Curious and yet beautiful it was to see little girls of seven or eight years, thus surprised at my approach, dash forward, even toward the advancing ogre, in order to snatch younger brothers or sisters left in their charge from unknown dangers. At a turn in the road I passed some boys bathing in a stream on the opposite shore, and at least a dozen rods away, but at the first sight of me they made for dry land and trooped away, naked, up the bank. At another place, while walking somewhat in advance, I came suddenly upon two pretty children, who, approaching from the opposite direction, were completely taken by surprise, and had no opportunity to escape. Their faces showed they were very much frightened, and the youngest clung closely to his brother. Just as I was about to speak, they made the most profound of reverences, withal so prettily, that I gave them each a penny, demonstrating, I hope, in their minds that even a white-faced barbarian is not dangerous if one is only polite. The word "boor" has no significance in Japan.

Our path suddenly turned upward into another valley facing a range of mountains, of a peculiar tooth-shaped and jagged character, and about three o'clock I reached a tea-house, where I decided to stay. The glare of the sun had given me a headache, and I prefer quiet to sight-seeing.

Mio-gi-San, August 11.—Slept but poorly, kept awake

by the greatest pest of Japan for a good part of the night. An old woman brought a lantern into my chamber after I had retired, and placed it at my head. "Take it away; I don't want it," I said. "Hai," she composedly replied, and left it burning. Was too tired to get up, and it burned all night. Why will they not comprehend my orders about meals? "Bring me," I say, in tolerable Japanese(?), "some hot water, two bowls, and some boiled rice." "Hai," says the servant, disappearing and returning after a long period with these articles and a complete array of Japanese dishes besides. Discovered on trial that some articles were at least palatable; one, a sort of pickled salmon, being quite good.

After breakfast I climbed the narrow street of this village leading to the shrine and temple. In this romantic spot, nearly a thousand years ago, a certain holy abbot sought a hermitage to mourn in secret the downfall of his favourite pupil. Here he died, and after death was deified as a Shinto god. With the instinct common to this race, the place became a favourite resort for pilgrims; and a temple in honour of the new deity was erected near the spot where as a poor hermit he doubtless passed many lonely days. The scenery about is singularly fine. "From the bosom of a gloomy grove rise innumerable pinnacles of rock, gradually increasing in height round a lofty central peak at least a thousand feet from base to summit."

I climbed the steps to the shrine, the solid stone

masonry reminding me of Nikko. Everything, however, is tending toward decay; the temples ill-kept, the shrines but little visited. It has lately undergone an official "purification" of every taint of Buddhism, and the shrine given over to the exclusive custody of Shinto priests. How it has improved by this action I cannot tell, but certainly, as a rule, I prefer even Buddhism and Buddhist temples to anything one sees in Shintoism. It is sometimes said in praise of Shintoism that one sees no images in its temples. It may be true, and the religion be of a low type notwithstanding. There are "no images" in the Mormon Temple at Salt Lake; is it worthy for that reason to be counted superior to Notre Dame? You enter a Shinto temple, and, instead of the magnificent shrine to Buddha, the eye rests first on a gigantic money-chest blocking up the doorway! Besides, even "purified Shintoism" has its images. Behind the temple, in a recess evidently visited by pilgrims now and then, were two hideous idols or faces of wood, one green and the other red, surrounded by votive offerings. What business have such images in a temple claiming to be purer than Buddha's shrines?

From my inn I could see far up the mountain-side a single projecting rock, crowned with a Chinese character. From a distance it looks as if painted white; but this appearance is said to be due solely to tiny strips of paper which different pilgrims have tied to the bamboos of which it is composed. I tried to reach it; but after following the steep path for half an hour it ended in the dry bed of a mountain stream, and this, followed still further, grew at last impassable. Turning to retrace my steps, I saw the great white symbol seemingly as far distant overhead as at setting out.

Going up, I passed one of those spider's webs which I have noticed previously, singular from the enormous length of the cables. This web was suspended between trees over fifteen feet apart, and very cleverly "guyed" to rocks underneath. While looking at it, a fly as large as a honey-bee tried to pass through the web with the usual entangling alliances, but no spider appeared. My desire to see this creature was rather stronger than inclination to interfere with "Nature's beautiful economy," so I left it undisturbed. On returning, found the centre of the web occupied by a huge spider as large as a tarantula, but no trace of the fly, who had doubtless fulfilled its "mission." Being touched with a stick, the creature dropped to the ground and pretended to be dead, but on turning away for a moment to seek some means of capturing it alive, it suddenly scampered into a hole, and I saw it no more. Its size, however, explains why the webs are so large and strong. When I reached the temple grounds it seemed to me that one of my feet was wet, though no water had been crossed. On examination I found the stocking soaked with blood, and three gorged leeches rolled out on the stone step. I had caught them somehow in the wood.

As I sat by the great stone Tori near the temple the chief priest sent his servant to invite me to his house. It was a plain wooden building, built, however, on a terrace of masonry at least fifty feet high on the outer face, commanding a magnificent prospect over the valley. Indeed, I think I have never seen a finer view from any private residence than that which one looks upon from the matted floor of this poor dwelling. A good telescope would make visible almost the entire plain between this place and Tokio. After usual salutations, I sat down on the floor, pipes were produced, followed by tea and bits of sponge cake, esteemed a great delicacy here in Japan. Conversation was of course limited. I produced my passport to satisfy natural curiosity; it told my name, route, and objects of travel. The beauty of the scenery was of course referred to. I made inquiries in regard to distances from this point to many others, and that was all. Coming again to the temple grounds, I saw a child looking over the edge of a stone bridge which crossed a mountain stream, and I approached to see the object at which it was gazing. It was a little Japanese maiden taking a bath in the clear, cool water, here forming a little pool at the foot of a cascade. She looked a veritable wood-nymph; a frightened nymph, too, when she saw me. I turned away, and presently saw her, nude, run up the bank, dress herself in that single garment which constitutes the apparel of a Japanese woman, and hurry away.

The afternoon was warm, and I took a nap. Awakened by the hostess, who, pushing aside the screen, came into the room with a bland smile as if about to confer a favour of unusual magnitude, and set down before me a glass filled with grated ice, water, and coarse brown sugar. Of course I didn't want it, and felt at liberty to say so. She could not comprehend the refusal. I must be mistaken as to its flavour, she thought; and taking up on a spoon a bit of the brown sugar, she offered it to me as one who gives a delicacy beyond price! It was only when I made her understand that it might give me a toothache that she comprehended, and, with a look of pity for my deprivation, drank it herself.

Towards evening a neighbouring guest came to my room, and after a few complimentary phrases, fell into questioning me on geography. He drew from memory a surprisingly accurate outline of the two hemispheres, and then pointed out England, and the location of other European countries and their capitals, seeking from me their foreign pronunciation.

In an adjoining room, a girl was teaching three children—the oldest nine, the youngest but six years of age—the graces and attitudes of a dancing girl. The children were quick learners. They flirted fan and waved handkerchief to the notes of a guitar, but it was not a pleasing sight to see children, not yet out of babyhood, thus imitating the languishing looks and ardours of love-sick maidenhood.

August 12.—After breakfast called for my bill, and ordered a pack-horse to be ready to take me to Sakamoto. The charges were very reasonable—eighty-three sen, or two shillings, for two days' board, and about eighteenpence additional for the horse. The dew was still on the grass when we started off, following a narrow path, which wound about at the foot of precipitous rocks towering a thousand feet above us. Indeed, it was apparently so little travelled that it seemed more like a path in some country pasture than a highway common to all. Spiders' webs particularly noticeable. I saw a very large web of the ordinary shape, but so finely spun that the threads around the centre were hardly a tenth of an inch equidistant.

We crossed several rustic bridges before striking into the Naka-sen-do, where, I regret to say, they are fast giving place to new structures of European patterns. An ancient Japanese bridge is as picturesque a structure as could be made of wood alone. It is generally arched somewhat in the middle, but the arch is often supported in the centre. However small or narrow it may be, earth is placed over the wood, and grass and flowers encouraged to grow on either side, so that except by noticing the stream below one would hardly know he were crossing a bridge—so like the roadside it is made to appear. The horse certainly does not seem to know when he leaves the path for the bridge, and as Japanese horses are very timorous, I have sometimes imagined the fashion of making bridges resemble the road has been invented to deceive the horse. Some of the older bridges are very manifestly unsafe, at least to my notion. I have crossed over torrents forty feet below, by bridges, the decay of whose timbers was distinctly visible; but there is no denying their picturesque beauty. Before Japan replaces them all with bright new painted structures, I hope some artist will have transferred a few of them to his canvas.

After reaching the Naka-sen-do, a further journey of two miles brought me to Saka-moto, at the foot of the Usui pass. I wanted the man to go further, but he would not be tempted. As a rule, owners of pack-horses will not go over eight or ten miles away from home; to go on one must make another engagement. My coolie, whose wages unfortunately had been paid in advance, set me down with all my luggage at the first eating-house in town, and turned homeward. I asked the landlord the charge for another animal over the pass to Karuizawa, on the opposite slope, a distance of seven miles. He went out to inquire, and on returning told me a yen and a half. This was evidently an imposition. It was yet early in the day; I was in no special hurry, and after trying without avail to make the pack-horse owner lower his charge, I concluded to find what the just charge should be by applying to the police.

Half-way up the village street was the police-office. A rude, unpainted wooden table, with three chairs, was the sole furniture of the little room open to the street. Two young men, dressed in white cotton duck jackets and trousers, constituted the visible force. I stated my business in a jumble of Japanese words which they were good enough to comprehend. Was the price too much? Neither would commit himself on this point, but one was ordered by his superior to accompany me back to the inn, and the result was a charge of one yen, instead of one and a half. Mounting upon my pony, I expressed duly my thanks to the young official, who seemed on his part delighted to have had the opportunity of doing something.

The road up the pass is at an easy grade, the bed well constructed, and the windings in and out of picturesque ravines and round about jutting crests are as fine and as numerous as one could wish. The long procession of pack-horses and foot travellers, outlined against the sky far above us; the lengthening train below us, slowly marching in and out of the curving passage we had made half an hour or an hour before; Saka-moto, with its black-roofed houses and simple narrow street spread out like a map;—all this was novel as experience, and beautiful as a view. As we ascended still higher the scenery becomes more and more impressive. In respect to beauty it far surpasses the two Swiss passes I have crossed. At one point near the summit I counted five distinct ranges of hills or mountains, separated each by intervening valleys, all green with forest trees or plants, and each with a slightly varying tint peculiar to itself, due to the different distances which intervened. In Switzerland one not unfrequently sees two such ranges. At Berne I believe one may see three; but I never before saw five, arranged as I have described. As one looks upon such a view from such a place, he cannot help picturing in the mind the strange pageants which have crossed these mountains during the ten centuries it has been a royal road. Armies, going forth to battle, or retreating after defeat, have here passed in long defile; shoguns and mikados, myriads of pilgrims, and millions of humble peasants have toiled upward and passed onward into oblivion, each with his own particular joys and hopes, his burden of sorrows, disappointments and cares. We do not know their names; they are as nothing to us of to-day, even as our memories and our little lives shall be forgotten by the coming millions of a century hence.

The descent to Karuizawa on the opposite slope is very easy, and the scenery by no means equal to that of the ascent. We reached the town about two in the afternoon, tired and hungry. Found a tolerable inn, Kameya's, where a good room was allotted me looking upon a neat little garden, and here I spent the afternoon writing letters.

Towards evening the house began to fill up with guests, and the large room adjoining mine was given to a party of pilgrims in company with one or two priests.

Shortly after their arrival they began their devotions by hanging in a recess of the wall a picture painted on silk, representing, as nearly as I could make out, nothing but a bit of natural scenery, probably some sacred place. In front of this they knelt, bowed their heads reverently

THE WAYSIDE INN.

to the floor again and again, and began in concert a slow, measured, musical chant. Now and then it ceased, when the only sounds to be heard were the rattling of the rosaries, and the prolonged sibilant in-drawing of breath by which the Japanese express intensity of emphasis or emotion. Then all would again bow, slowly

A Cross-Country Excursion.

and reverently, until face touched the very floor. A moment later a single voice would begin the chant anew in a low and scarcely audible tone; another would join him, others would fall in, until again the measured rhythm would be repeated as before. Other travellers at the inn seem oblivious to their presence, so far as it suggests any necessity for silence or decorum. "'Tis the business of priests and pilgrims to chant prayers, but not ours to listen," they perhaps hold. I have just been to the front of the inn; the entrance is hung with numerous Chinese lanterns, and the proprietor stands near the door ready to welcome the coming guest.

CHAPTER X.

ON THE NAKA-SEN-DO.

Pilgrims and prayers—Supplications for a penny—Oiwake by coach—Provoking experiences—Apparently a mirage—Mochidzuke—Fun at my expense—The long Wada pass—New costumes—Shimo no Suwa—Japanese dogs—Inherent gentleness of the people—A pious landlord.

August 13.—Awakened during the night by what seemed to me distant music; it was only the pilgrims chanting prayers at midnight in a soft undertone. At daybreak they again awoke me by their morning worship, but I slept fully two hours after they had gone on their way. The weather looked a little threatening, and instead of going on by private conveyance I decided to take the public coach to Oiwake this afternoon.

Took a walk through the town, which is highly praised by the guide-book as a good resort for foreigners from Tokio, during the summer. A more dreary place, however, to my notion, it would be hard to imagine.

On the Naka-sen-do.

Only a few miles distant is Asama-Yama, one of the largest active volcanoes in Japan. It seems about as high as Vesuvius, and with my glass I can easily distinguish a portion of the crater, with great volumes of smoke and vapour pouring out. Apparently it is not more than five or six miles from here to its base, but appearances are often deceptive as regards such intervening spaces. While I was looking at it from the edge of the village, a number of children, chiefly boys, gathered about me, displaying less fear than is customary.

Presently I noticed a couple of Buddhist pilgrim-beggars going from house to house, evidently receiving alms and rendering payment in some sort of ceremony resembling prayers. Indicating to a small boy that I wished one brought, he dashed up the street and soon returned, followed by a sturdy pilgrim. His costume was different in colour from that worn by Japanese generally, being of a bluish-grey, while about the neck he wore a large white canvas bag inscribed with Chinese characters, into which he dropped whatever was given him. I presented him with two sen (about three farthings), and immediately he began with closed eyes to recite rapidly a sort of litany, in which the word "Nam-i-yo" had considerable part. In his hands he carried a little gong, upon which he tapped from time to time, as if keeping therewith a tally of his prayers. The children grouped themselves around us; passing travellers stopped to look; their pack-horses found their way to the grass by the wayside; the neighbours left their work and joined the group; and still with closed eyelids the pilgrim repeated his invocations or prayers. I must have largely overpaid him, for he certainly favoured me with twice as many prayers as he gave to anybody else.

About two o'clock in the afternoon, while I was enjoying a noonday siesta, the coach came rattling to the door of the inn, and before I was fairly awakened we were zig-zagging along the road in a crazy vehicle filled with Japanese, all but the front seat, which I shared with the driver. The poor beast had seen its best days as a steady-going pack-horse, and now was only to be kept to a slow and heavy trot by continual use of the whip. The shouts of the driver were incessant, and with all his urging the pace was slow. Reached Oiwake about five, and found without difficulty a clean and respectable appearing inn.

August 14.—Awoke about two o'clock this morning with a sense of oppressed breathing, and stepped out on the porch facing the garden. The moon was shining in full splendour, and by its light I saw a great spider weaving his web between the two wooden pillars upholding the roof. It did not observe me, and busily crossed from side to side. One of its cable-threads, which I found attached to the side of the house and reaching thence to the web, was so strong that it permitted my finger to slide up and down it as though it were a silken thread, which indeed in one sense it was.

On the Naka-sen-do. 103

When I got up this morning, however, the night's industry had been destroyed by the busy housemaid.

A provoking experience with the landlord regarding conveyance to the next stopping-place. I thought, and still believe, that last evening I distinctly engaged two karumas at a definite price for the journey; but on asking for them after breakfast, I was told none were to be had, and that I must travel by pack-horse. There was nothing to be done; the horse was awaiting me at the door, and I took it, although angry afterwards at myself for so doing. The beast was provokingly slow; it ambled along, snatching its breakfast as it went from the grass and shrubs at the wayside. Once a mail-coach came clattering by, so scaring it that it rushed out of the road into the adjoining field, to the great danger of its rider. At another time its owner very cleverly quickened its pace by holding wisps of grass just in front of its nose and beyond its grasp. It was too lazy to trot after them, but the manœuvre sensibly accelerated its speed for a time. For the greater part of the way I preferred walking to such a steed.

Just before reaching the next village, Otai, and while it was still early, we had a rare view of the distant mountains, with all the appearance of a mirage or optical illusion. While descending a long hill, I saw in the distance the continuation of this road disappearing in a vague horizon of clouds, above which, floating as it were in the sky, was an extensive landscape, forests, fields, and villages ending in another horizon. At first I thought it was a veritable mirage, but as we continued it became more distinct; that which seemed to be the first horizon was merely a cloud floating in the valley, and intercepting or dividing the landscape in two.

The ride was monotonous, and I found little interest in the villages through which we passed. At one place, it is true, a peasant had trained a pumpkin vine to grow over his little arbour, and the huge vegetables dangled over the heads of the idlers below. I saw a blind woman making her way homeward, carrying in both hands a heavy sack of coals; and yet by means of the staff she carried, together with her perfect knowledge of the road, she got along without difficulty, crossed the gutter, and turned without aid into her own house. That she was quite blind was perceptible from her method of progression, and from the fact that she missed the door of the house to which she was going by about three feet. The wonder was that she could find it at all, and, with both hands filled, manage so cleverly to pick her way. Her face was very pretty; it had, moreover, a peculiarly peaceful expression that I have noticed frequently in the blind, especially in this country; the reflection of an inward contentment, which nature sometimes kindly allots when she deprives us of her greatest gifts.

Reached Mochidzuki shortly after noon, tired, dusty, and with a headache. The principal inn refused to entertain strangers or was already full, and I was therefore compelled to put up at a second-rate inn, where the total accommodation was but two rooms, of which I have the best. Went out for a walk through the village, and on returning found a party of travellers in the other room. The afternoon was very warm; there was little or no wind stirring, and the landlady by signs requested that I permit the screens to be removed so as to allow of as much circulation of air as possible. I did so, and the result was that I occupied one-half of a large room during the rest of my stay.

A little comedy was enacted in the street opposite my door. A naked boy, seven or eight years old, refused to be scrubbed in the stream flowing through the village, and resisted with tooth and nail. A crowd, largely of youthful sympathizers, gathered about him. The women, however, berate him soundly, and his mother administers most emphatic condemnation of his obstinacy. It ended in his being by main force duly washed, in spite of constant screaming and much ill-directed effort.

August 15.—Where yesterday ended and to-day's record began is somewhat uncertain in my mind. I have had a night's experience in a poor inn; it is good enough for a single occasion, but one does not desire frequent repetitions. Shortly after nine o'clock in the evening my hostess brought in the usual supply of bedding, but having some suspicions in regard to it, I made my single blanket answer instead for bed and coverlet. My companions, a few feet distant, made merry until a much later hour; and I could not but compare my tranquillity in this heathen country in such a place, with my probable feeling if, equally ignorant of the language and unprotected, I were passing the night in some rustic inn of Italy, Greece, or Spain. Sleep was impossible or nearly so; the pest of Japan which murders slumber attacked with vigour. Some time after midnight I was awakened by the clapping of hands. "Hai," said the landlord from an adjoining room. An order was then given by one of the travellers in the other compartment, and I presently heard him stirring about, waking his wife, and lighting a lamp, which he brought into our room. It seemed to me it could not possibly be daybreak. I looked at my watch; it was just 2.30 a.m. Nevertheless there was no mistake about one matter—everybody in the inn was astir, and further sleep was impossible. The hostess lit a fire and commenced preparations for breakfast; the pilgrim recited his prayers with much repetition of words and rubbing of beads, while the other travellers went on with conversation as if he were not present. Soon the baby of the family, an unlovely, inquisitive boy of from four or five but yet unweaned, roused itself into wakefulness and caused to vanish at once every vision of further slumber on my part. He came to the edge of my mosquito net and wished to enter; but somewhere one must draw the line where familiarity shall cease, and I draw it at babies at three o'clock in the morning. His mother was more successful as an inquisitor. While the travellers were breakfasting she persisted in coming to my mat to ask questions, and then going back to the guests to repeat my answers for their amusement. For instance, I had arranged for a horse this morning to Wada for a yen and a half. There was nothing disputable or questionable in the bargain. This was no hindrance. Assuming an innocent air, she would kneel down where I was trying to woo unconsciousness and shout, "Donna-sama!" until I opened my eyes. Nobody ever before called me "Donna-sama." I fancy, however, it is a term of respect. "What do you want?" I cried, somewhat irritably I fear. "Donna-sama— uma — Wada — ichi yen go-ju sen" (Sir, a horse, Wada, one yen and fifty sen), repeating the words as originally stated. "Hai, yo-roshiu" (yes, all right), I replied, repeating after her the phrase. Then back again to her guests, where I could not but hear my tones and accents outrageously imitated to their delight, if laughter was any proof. Singularly she never seemed to imagine that I could understand her mimicry; for the innate politeness of Japanese, I am confident, would prevent all intentional or careless discourtesy. Half a dozen times at least she disturbed me to ask some question or other, and returned to repeat my replies, until even the naked baby took up the refrain and lisped before me, "Donny-oo-ma-ichi yen?"

By four o'clock breakfast had been eaten, and both pilgrims and travellers had departed on their way. To hope for rest was quite useless, and I concluded to get off as early as possible. By five o'clock the horse was at my door, and soon afterwards the village was behind us. The morning was cool but pleasant. Passing through village after village alike uninteresting, we reached Naga-kubo, where, if I had been wise, I should have come last night. It is a very pleasant village, with peach trees planted on either side of the street, a peculiarity not elsewhere seen up to this point. I noticed also that brighter colours are now beginning to be in vogue; strips of scarlet appear as lining to the blue sleeves of the maidens, and they themselves, if I am not mistaken, are of better features than their more northern sisters.

"Wada," says the guide-book, "is a poor village," and consequently I arranged my plans so as not to stop there over night. But even the best authorities are human—a reflection which came to mind when the guide set me down in Wada at the cleanest, largest, and best-seeming inn I have yet seen in Japan. It was, however, too early in the day to think of stopping for the night, especially as the weather was fine, and the highest mountain pass on the Naka-sen-do before us. I rested an hour, took some lunch, and engaged another horse to take me to the summit of the pass.

On asking my account of the landlord on taking leave,

On the Naka-sen-do. 109

a characteristic little comedy occurred, which the actors doubtless thought unintelligible to me. The hostess was standing near, and in a very audible "aside" I heard her whisper, "Ni-ju sen" (about sixpence). The price was by no means unreasonable, considering that I had occupied the best room for an hour, served with dishes, hot water, and rice newly cooked without stint. But nevertheless it was an exorbitant price for Japan, and the husband, landlord though he was, had not the heart to say it. Words passed between them; I fancied he was remonstrating with the too-thrifty housewife for her grasping disposition. It ended by his saying, "Ju sen," or one-half the price she had suggested. This was not the only occasion in which a woman has proposed to a reluctant husband a demand for a double price.

Another horse was engaged, and we were off before noon. The road leads up the mountain by a narrow valley, every arable part of which is cultivated; irrigation being easily accomplished by means of the numerous mountain streams. My coolie was disposed to be talkative, and would not or could not comprehend my repeated assertions, "Nippon kotobade zonji masen" (Japanese language I don't understand). It is a curious circumstance that country people who rarely see foreigners, everywhere seem unable to comprehend their inability to speak their language. I remember once riding in a rustic stage-coach in the Thüringian forest shortly after going to Germany, when an old peasant began talking to me. "I don't understand German," I said to him, using one of the phrases the traveller first learns. "Warum?" said the old man, looking me earnestly in the face as if to find there the reason of my confessed stupidity. It is needless to say I could not answer his inquiry and explain "why." The country people in Japan sometimes are equally inquisitive. After I had replied to my coolie's observations in the set form as above several times without any effect, I took the easier method of saying "no" or "yes," calculating as far as possible, by his tones, which answer he expected or preferred. As he seemed quite satisfied with the arrangement I had no reason to complain.

We stopped to rest, a few rods below the summit of the pass, at an excellent tea-house, and as it looked as if a storm were probable, I concluded to go no further. My last night's experience did not dispose me to any needless or prolonged journeyings.

The baths in Japanese houses are curious; they are always wooden, and usually resemble half a hogshead. In some way not quite easy to understand, the water is heated by a small stove under the bath itself. Except when one is sure of being the first to arrive, it is more satisfactory to have a tub, for there is no change of water no matter how many there are to bathe. Probably the custom does not seem to the Japanese so outrageous as to us, since everybody bathes every day as regularly as he eats his dinner.

On the Naka-sen-do.

August 16.—Climbed to the top of the hill by the pass after breakfast, whence a magnificent view of the surrounding country was obtained, the principal peaks of the central mountains being nearly all visible. No horses or conveyances being procurable, I engaged a coolie who agreed to carry my traps to the village of Shima-no-Suwa, about seven miles distant, for forty sen, about a shilling. The road was downhill the entire distance, but for most of the way it led through a narrow gorge, devoid of views. Going through a village I met a curious little procession, consisting evidently of three generations—an old woman, her daughter, and grandchild. Each had something in her hands; the child carried a stick of incense, which had been lighted. They turned out of the road into a cemetery by the village temple, and I followed them. In one corner was a new-made grave, perhaps that of the husband of the younger woman. Upon the tombstone they placed offerings of rice and other articles of food, poured liberal libations of tea upon the grave, while the baby placed the lighted incense in front of the headstone.

We reached the town of Shimo-no-Suwa just as it was beginning to rain. The hotel to which I first applied, the "Ki-kio-ya," refused to take foreigners, which does not speak well for their experience with Europeans. Another was so full of pilgrims and travellers that it was quite uninviting, as evidently there was no accommodation for a traveller wishing a room to himself. Found finally a fair second-rate inn, Kam-e-ya's, where I was given a large room upstairs. There is a long window overlooking the street, but the light is obscured by wooden bars two inches apart, for which I can imagine no use except possibly in stormy or wintry weather, to break the force of the wind against the paper window-panes within.

Notwithstanding the summer showers, I started after dinner for a walk about the town. It is situated near the Lake of Suwa, and is noted for its hot baths, to which numbers of afflicted resort from the surrounding country. The water is quite warm, over 113° F., and is reputed to contain silver—a reputation which in the eyes of the Japanese vastly enhances its curative properties. Nearly every house on the main street has its bath; but why those of hotels should be projected into the street like a portico, compelling publicity, is not exactly clear, unless it be for advertising purposes.

Found my way to a Shinto temple where a curious ceremony was in progress. Fronting a long kagura stage, built for the "sacred dances" so denominated, was another building, quite empty, about the porticos of which a number of children were romping. Between this building, possibly a shrine, and the long kagura platform, was a broad paved walk, about twenty feet wide, and along this about thirty girls, fifteen to twenty years of age, were passing to and fro, stopping at either terminus a few moments to repeat prayers. They did tyrannical, bullying spirit, so often observed among boys of England and America, that delight in inflicting pain or ignominy on weaker companions, out of mere love of exercising brute force. Japanese children are all well behaved, not merely towards foreigners or their elders, but even towards each other, and it is always pleasant to see them at play, where one can do so unobserved. In practical conformity to the teachings of Jesus Christ, in gentleness, in meekness, in a willingness to bear evil rather than do evil, the Japanese are to-day more really a Christian nation than any people of Europe or America.

After sundown, on going out, I found the entire street lighted by tiny bonfires, made of two or three bits of some resinous bark. The idea seemed to be to make as many little fires as possible, instead of one large blaze, and each child (for it was all the play of children) was busily engaged in tending his own illumination, and watching the success of others. It was a very pretty sight, the long street thus illuminated, and the parents sitting in front of their homes seemed to enjoy it as much as their children.

On returning to the inn, the landlord offered to give me a better room, partly, I suspect, because the one I had is suitable for a number of pilgrim guests. The one to which I was transferred I found very pleasant; quite apart from the main part of the inn; in fact, I believe it is the landlord's own room. It looks directly upon a little courtyard, not much over twelve feet square, wherein Japanese taste has contrived a very pretty little garden; a tiny fountain gushing out of rocks, a pond with gold-fish swimming about, ferns and flowers. In a corner of the garden are the shrines of two gods of good luck; and, judging from appearances, they seem to have favoured my Japanese host. He is a pious man, for, within-doors, near my room, I see a gilded statue of Buddha, wrapped in contemplation. Before it burns continually a little lamp. And listening again to the low chanting of the pilgrims, I go off to sleep.

CHAPTER XI.

THE MOUNTAIN REGION.

The Shiwo-jiri Pass—Peculiar house architecture—A country bridge—Visit to Matsumoto—An inhospitable town—Return to Shiwo-jiri—Walk to Niyegawa—Mysteries of a magnifying-glass—Letter of introduction given—Hirosawa—Picturesque village—Singular female costume—Village industries—Beasts of burden.

August 17.— Pilgrims are a nuisance. Their early departure inevitably makes morning slumbers impossible in any inn patronized by them. For breakfast I was given a new dish, a sort of soup made of tiny shell-fish resembling fresh-water clams; they were cooked in their shells, but I found them very nice, despite a sauce which was intended to give the universal flavour of native cookery. Soon after breakfast I mounted the pack-horse, and started for Shiwo-jiri Pass. For the first mile or two the path was nearly level, winding about through rice patches and peasant villages. As we ascended the mountain-side, the beauty of the scenery increased, and from the summit a very fine view was obtained of the valley in which lies the lake of Suwa, with the villages that cluster along its banks, and the mountain-peaks in the distance. I saw one upon which, with my glass, I could quite clearly distinguish long streaks of snow lying in drifts on the mountain-side, but not covering the top.

I have especially noticed to-day the taste displayed by the Japanese, where utility only is the object aimed at in some other countries. In America, for instance, in the rural districts, a drinking-trough for horses by the roadside is almost always a log, hollowed, and often decaying after it has been long in use. About this district they are invariably of stone. Sometimes a large boulder will be selected from the bed of a torrent, and a deep, square basin hewn out of it. Then, with much labour, it is moved into a position where some clear rill may be conducted into it, and there it remains for centuries. Stone walls, also, enclosing rice-fields, or the grounds belonging to temples, are almost always beautiful specimens of masonry. The corners usually have that singular fashion which makes them resemble nothing so much as the steel prow of a modern ironclad, projecting outward at the base, and curving upward and inwards. The stones at the corners even of country partition walls are laid in the same fashion as those of fortifications, an upward slant inwards apparently giving additional strength. The mason work of the Japanese is always excellent, and, as

I have thought a hundred times, it is an infinite pity that they had not followed the fashion of other nations in constructing their temples of stone. Can it be that frequency of earthquakes has made wood structures preferable?

Most of the houses are thatched with straw; but along the ridge is quite frequently a hanging garden of grass and flowers, very pretty indeed, when birds are seen nesting among them. Even a little foot-bridge, four or five feet long, spanning a roadside brook, is contrived with an idea for beauty as well as use. In country districts of America, the working man would be content to throw a plank or two across the stream, wide enough to permit passage, and strong enough to bear the weight of an ordinary man. Of beauty in such an affair he has not the least concept. Quite different is the Japanese idea; he wants a structure equally serviceable, but he wants it to be beautiful as well. He therefore imitates in miniature a large bridge. First, piles are driven into the bank at the water's edge; behind them, placed, however, horizontally, is another row of fagots, so as to strengthen and support those in front. From one such embankment to the other sticks of wood are laid and fastened down; the whole is covered with earth; the edges of the little bridge are bordered with grass and flowers and overhanging plants; and in the end one has a footway equally strong and serviceable, and far prettier than one built with utility only in view.

Of these tiny bridges the Japanese are very fond; there is something in a bridge itself, use aside, which in the peasant's eyes enhances the picturesque quality of landscape. I saw to-day a tiny bamboo bridge spanning the roadside streamlet which ran in front of a poor man's cottage. Over the framework of bamboo he had trained a running flower-vine, a sort of "morning glory;" the flowers and leaves almost completely hid their support, and seemed of themselves to span the running stream. In the garden of the house where I am writing, over a swift streamlet that passes through, an evergreen shrub has been trained to grow in the form of a bridge.

Arrived at Shiwo-jiri about noon, and found an excellent inn, at which I was tempted to stop. The large city of Matsumoto lies about ten miles off the route, and I determined to visit it, to spend the night there, and to return here to-morrow. After some time I managed to make the landlord understand my wishes in regard to storage of luggage, and engaging a jinrikisha, we were off shortly after one o'clock. The road to Matsumoto lies in a fertile valley, with mountains in the distance on either side. We crossed a broad moor, where, in 1583, a celebrated battle was fought. *Cui bono?* The traveller does not even know why they fought, and yet, doubtless, they who died believed it was for their country and their gods.

Matsumoto was reached in about two hours, as my coolie stopped but once to rest on the way. Arriving

The Mountain Region. 121

in town, I went from inn to inn, only to find it impossible to obtain accommodation. Foreigners were not desired at any price. In this dilemma I concluded to keep my coolie, and with him to see as much of the town as was possible in an afternoon, returning to Shiwo-jiri again towards night.

The "sights" of a provincial town like this one are not numerous or very remarkable; it is rather the people themselves that chiefly interest me. I like to stroll at leisure along the streets, buying trifles, or watching men and women at work; and such opportunity, to be enjoyable, must be combined with abundant time. As I saw it, Matsumoto seemed to be a prosperous town; it has, I believe, about fourteen thousand inhabitants. In enterprise the common people are exceedingly lacking in one respect. For example, I bought some peaches for which I was asked twopence; tendered a bit of money valued at fivepence, and the vendor preferred to fail in the bargain rather than make change. At another corner I saw some curious old beads for which the owner asked twenty sen. I offered him script for fifty sen, and exactly the same experience recurred; he had no change, and if a bystander had not given me the amount I wanted, the man would have preferred to allow the bargain to fall through rather than go and seek for smaller currency.

Accompanied by my jinrikisha-man, I found my way to the Buddhist temple of Sho-gio-ji, once probably of considerable importance, but not much patronized at present, since all the doors were closed, and no priest visible or to be found. As I went into the yard, the great bell was tolling. The bell-ringer was a young lad, in training evidently for a Buddhist priest. Bells in Japan are very clear and pure in tone; the method of ringing them is, however, quite different from ours. The bell is struck on the outside by a heavy wooden beam, so hung from the roof that, standing underneath it, the bell-ringer, with a long rope, can project the beam with considerable force against the outer rim of the bell. After watching the process for a time, I asked the little priest-boy to let me ring it a while, and the request being accompanied with a few coppers, he readily assented. Seizing the rope with considerably more force than was really necessary, I gave a peal that must have been heard in the surrounding country for miles. The beam of course rebounded, and, to my consternation, returning, gave another and lesser peal, quite out of rhythm, which must have proven to all who were listening that a new hand was at the rope.

Toward evening we started again for Shiwo-jiri, which was reached a little after sundown. The stout fellow had carried me nearly twenty-five miles, including our rambles about the town, and his demands—a yen and a half, about five shillings—were far from being unreasonable. In my absence, I found the landlord had assigned my room to guests, under the supposition that

I should not return. The house was now quite full, but he very cheerfully gave up his own quarters for my accommodation.

August 18.—As the road was picturesque and the day pleasant, I concluded to walk, and hired, therefore, but one karuma for my luggage. The scenery was fair, the road winding part of the way by the brink of a river, but at a considerable distance above it. About eleven o'clock it was exceedingly warm, and when the point to which I had engaged my karuma—the village of Niyegawa—was reached about noon, I concluded to go no further, but spend the day in writing letters. I passed the afternoon, therefore, at a pleasant tea-house, but, as night drew near, it became evident that they had no accommodation for guests, and I went out to seek for a hotel. Why I am refused at so many hotels I cannot understand, unless it be that foreigners, by their treatment of the natives, have earned an unenviable reputation. My search seemed to be in vain; the last and best inn had refused me; but when I assured them that I did not care for any food, and wished only lodging, they assented and took me in. It was a very quiet and respectable inn, evidently of a much higher grade than those patronized by pilgrims. The landlady and her maid came to my room, ostensibly to see if I wanted anything, but, I suspect, quite out of curiosity. They were both greatly pleased with my little "linen-counter" lens; the maid saw that no better object could be procured than a flea, and without ceremony began to search for one on her own person! I need hardly say that her industry was almost instantly rewarded.

Toward evening guests began to fill the house; they were all more quiet and better dressed than the pilgrim class with which I have so largely associated hitherto. Nevertheless, I cannot say that I liked them the better; certainly they were not their superiors in good breeding. A traveller would enter into conversation with the utmost politeness, inquire the stranger's nationality and destination, and be extremely civil so long as in my presence, but the moment he had rejoined his companions I could overhear him mimicking my intonations and mispronunciations of Japanese words, to the infinite amusement of his fellow-travellers. I hardly think this was intentional rudeness; it was rather the ignorance of all common people of the extent to which a foreigner can comprehend them, when he seems wholly ignorant of their language. A good supper was brought to me, notwithstanding my offer to accept lodging only, and a bed, larger and softer than any I have had for a long time, was spread out on the matted floor.

Friday, August 19.—I heard the clock strike five this morning, but no one was stirring about the house, except myself, until nearly six. Evidently, where pilgrims are not guests, the hours of rising are much later; indeed, the front doors, or wooden screens, were not opened until after breakfast. When I paid my reckoning—half a yen—the landlady inquired where I intended to stop to-night, and being told Agematsu, she gave me a note of introduction to some inn there—very gracious, I thought, considering she had at first refused me accommodation altogether. It was nearly seven o'clock before breakfast was finished, and, with a stout porter bearing my luggage on his back, I was on my way up the valley. After a walk of two miles, we came to Hirosawa, a picturesque little village, all the inhabitants of which seem devoted to the manufacture of lacquer work. Every house on the main street is not only a home, but a manufactory and a shop. A mile or two beyond comes the village of Narai at the foot of the pass, where the same industry is carried on and a new one begun, that of making wooden combs. One sees the process better, however, on the other side of the mountain.

I noticed a peculiar dress worn by both sexes in a portion of this valley, quite unlike anything elsewhere in Japan to be observed. It consists of a pair of large Turkish trousers, very "baggy" till just above the knee, and then closely fitting the lower part of the limb. The fashion is peculiarly local, and is well adapted, of course, for a people living in a mountainous region. Going up the pass, we met two young girls descending, each not only leading a pack-horse laden with lumber, but carrying on her own back at least a hundredweight of planks. My guide addressed them with some familiarities which caused the first to smile, but as the second looked severely indignant, I am afraid his remarks were not courteous.

Stopped at a tea-house to let the coolie rest. The tea furnished is generally such weak stuff that one drinks it only for lack of something better. I wanted some coppers, but the cunning proprietor would give me nothing smaller than ten-sen script, knowing that they must be used at least to that amount to fee him. As I did not propose to fee him so exorbitantly for sitting down, I bought some *saké*, or rice-wine, for the coolie, and treated him to all the refreshments they had given me. About a mile further up the mountain the cunning rogue of a porter professed weariness, and stopped again at a tea-house. Here, too, the attempt to get smaller change than script was useless; they had none, although a constant stream of pilgrims and travellers are passing over the road, and pay nothing but coppers. There was no escape from paying, as a fee for sitting down, a sum almost as large as a pilgrim pays for a night's lodging and food, and I see now why the guide-book suggests "plenty of small change."

The view from the top of the pass is one of the best I have seen in Japan, chiefly because one looks so directly down upon villages and cultivated fields, lying far below, and yet apparently within stone's-throw. At one point on the summit, where, on a clear day, the sacred mountain, Ontake-San, may be just discerned, a shrine has been erected, a huge granite Torii, which gives the name to the pass. Besides the Torii, which generally symbolizes a Shinto shrine, there are numerous stone and bronze statues of Buddha and other deities erected here. It puzzles one, this combination of the symbols of two opposing religions. It is as if one saw the cross and the crescent on the same steeple.[1]

I should think that quite two-thirds (and perhaps three-fourths) of all the travellers one meets in this region are going on some pilgrimage. Their object is plainly enough told by their dress, which is white, rather than the favourite colour, blue, and by the sacred symbols and tinkling bells which they carry with them. The "high places" are especially sacred. Every mountain-top is reverenced, more, perhaps, for some deity or saint whose presence has made it sacred, than for itself. Even where, as at this point, only the distant peak of a particularly holy mountain can be occasionally discerned, a shrine is erected, and pilgrims passing stop to gaze and worship. Probably place-worship is as universal an instinct as hero-worship; pilgrims of old upon first sighting Santiago in Spain, uncovered, and proceeded, some upon their knees, to the holy city. The singular thing about Japan is that nearly every mountain or remarkable object of nature has come to be associated with some religious sentiment. I noticed, by the way, a curious picture, pasted as a charm against the door-

[1] This is actually the case in Russia; but the cross is above the crescent, and signifies its victory over it.

post of a house at Narai; it was a rude wood-cut copy of some European picture of the devil—the black man—with horns, hoofs, and forked tail. It may have been a copy of something introduced by the Jesuits three centuries ago, but I have never seen others elsewhere in Japan.

Yagohara, the village in the valley on the other side of Torii Pass, is almost exclusively devoted to the manufacture of wooden combs. It is a delicate kind of work, requiring a good eye, and a fair degree of manual dexterity. Upon an oblong bit of prepared wood, about the size of the comb that is to be, the workman first traces a line denoting its more precise shape, and a corresponding inner line to which the teeth are to be cut. Then fastening the wood in a little vice, with a fine saw he rapidly cuts the teeth, equidistant, and so far as can be seen, quite as accurately as could be done by machinery. They work with great rapidity; with my watch I counted twenty-eight teeth cut in a minute. As at Hirosawa, all the houses where they are made are shops for selling them; and the entire profit of the labour goes thus to the workman and his family. Of course, as Japan becomes "civilized," this will doubtless be changed; such work will be carried on in large establishments, and while the condition of the hand-labourer will perhaps be no better, Capital will secure a larger share of the profits. To doubt that this will be an improvement, is it not to question the advantages of civilization?

At Miya-no-Koshi, the next village through which we passed, a sort of religious festival was in progress. Every house was decorated by a long bamboo pole tied to the front door-posts to which streamers of parti-coloured paper were attached. At certain distances on the street, a kind of frame overhung the road, in which was suspended a number of large Chinese lanterns; the effect must have been rather pretty by night, when they were all lighted. Only the largest towns appear to light the streets for the use of the general public at night. In country places and villages there is not even a single lantern to be seen, except as pertaining to some private individual. All honest folk are doubtless supposed to retire early, and as all the people *are* honest, why keep up a useless light?

About four o'clock in the afternoon we reached the town of Fukushima, a good-sized place of nearly three thousand inhabitants, situated on both sides of the river Kiso-gawa. Altogether it seemed so pleasant that I determined to stay here, if possible, overnight. Past experiences were again repeated, however; the chief hotels respectfully but firmly declined to afford accommodation, and it was only after application to the police head-quarters that a room was obtained in a second-class inn. I could of course have gone on to Agematsu, five miles beyond, but the scenery about here was so pretty that I wanted to enjoy it at leisure.

After supper, I took a stroll about the town. It consists of two long straggling streets on either side of the river; two villages, in fact, united by large bridges. Most of the inns were filled with pilgrims, and shops for the sale of bells and beads, and plans of sacred places were very abundant. I saw one aged pilgrim going from door to door, repeating prayers or chanting litanies, and jingling at intervals a number of bronze rings, set into a curiously fashioned bronze handle. At the richer houses, a small coin would be given; at the poorest cottages, the housewife would bring a large handful of uncooked rice, and put it in the little bag which he carried hung about his neck. One could not but be reminded of Buddha, as he returned a mendicant to the palace of his royal father.

Crossing the river by a well-built bridge, I passed from the main road into the more secluded part of the town, and came at length to the village temple. The gates, as usual, were guarded by huge wooden statues of a most terrible-looking god, Em-ma, the Regent of the Hells, and the final judge of all male sinners. It is a fearful object, but I doubt whether one can deny to its influence some degree of good effects. That terrible face, into whose lineaments the artist has put every imaginable expression conducing to excite fear, glaring down from a darkened recess, may it not have kept many a hand from secret crime, or frightened many a sinner into restitution of goods wrongfully acquired? I lie down night after night, alone, unprotected, accessible to thief or assassin; yet without fear, without even taking the trouble to keep a loaded revolver within reach. There are many Christian countries in which a traveller would run greater risks to life and property by travelling alone in this manner. I should hardly care to do it in Southern Italy, or Greece, or some parts of Western America. For myself, I am very glad my Japanese hosts are neither Agnostics nor Secularists, but have, on the contrary, a very definite faith in the existence and watchfulness of their numerous deities, and a wholesome fear of future punishment after death for their most secret sins.

Beyond and behind the temple is the village cemetery; it is on a hillside overlooking the town. All the headstones were quite small, except one single row of solemn-looking granite monuments, that must mark the tombs of a great family. Some of them were apparently very old, at least two or three centuries, judging by comparison with other monuments of that period which I have seen elsewhere. The last-erected monument was of a far more modern style, and was quite covered with Chinese characters cut into the granite and gilded.

Returning through the village, a series of incidents occurred, all repetitions of what I have before described. A group of children playing in the street scattered in every direction at my approach; one remained behind to rescue her baby brother, and I was at her side before she could get away! I gave her a few coppers that the others might see what they had possibly lost through their fear. A little beyond this, two girls came out to a well to draw water, and when they saw me I was between the house and the well. When they saw their chances of escape were really cut off, a look of absolute terror came into their faces, and then followed a low bow, which was duly returned on my part, and I passed on, doubtless to their great relief. A number of the townspeople gathered about their doors to observe my movements. I showed some of them my opera-glass, and judging from their exclamations of wonder, pleasure, and surprise, I should imagine that the most of them had never even heard of so marvellous an instrument. Crossing the bridge, I saw a number of naked boys bathing in the stream below; they were greatly frightened at my watching them through the glass, and scrambled to the bank, and away out of sight as soon as possible.

Returning to the inn, found the street nearly blocked by a dozen huge bulls (here used as beasts of burden) belonging to some carriers who had stopped to refresh themselves. The feet were shod with straw sandals like those of horses; all were carrying heavy loads; some, indeed, were lying down and chewing the cud of apparent contentment under a load of several hundred pounds. They are doubtless worked too hard to be at all savage in disposition, and certainly they mind the directions of their drivers far better than most oxen I have seen elsewhere.

CHAPTER XII.

IN THE HEART OF JAPAN.

Agematsu—Magnificent scenery—Mountain mills—Village processions and dancing dragons—The artist in dough—Call from the schoolmaster—Lightning rods upon telegraph-poles—At whose suggestion?—Isumago—Magome Pass—On a pack-horse—A narrow bridge—Led by a woman—Oi—Comforts of Japanese inns.

Agematsu, August 20.—A walk of two hours along one of the finest bits of mountain road I have ever seen, brought me to this place, where I shall remain a day or two. Went at once to the inn, to the proprietor of which I had the introductory note given me. No contrast could be greater than my reception here and my experience elsewhere. The host met me at the door, read my note, and then dropped on his knees and saluted me with forehead to the dust. I responded with the lowest bow a Western barbarian could possibly bring himself to make, which gratified him so much that he repeated his obeisance, this time keeping his forehead for several seconds against the floor. The best room was assigned me; from some place, perhaps the police-station, a very inky table and a plain wooden chair were borrowed, the host placing them in my room with the air of a man conscious of knowing the requirements of civilized life. When, in addition to my usual plain repast, he added two or three fresh-caught and newly-cooked brook trout, I felt inclined to stay here a week.

After dinner, about three o'clock, I walked down the valley to an old Buddhist monastery, where a very pretty bit of natural scenery is to be enjoyed. The river contracted by rocky banks within a current scarcely eighteen feet wide, rushes through with a swiftness that reminds one of the rapids above Niagara. Indeed, the Japanese are very enthusiastic in their praise of this view. One of their guide-books says that "its noble character can scarcely be appreciated by the mind, nor adequately described in language." We should hardly be more enthusiastic in praise of the " noble character " of Niagara itself.

Returning to the village by a side path, I heard, in passing by a little stream, a monotonous and regular splashing of water, accompanied by a heavy *thud*. Going nearer to the sound, I found a curious specimen of Japanese water-power at work, not grinding, but *pounding* grain into meal. The method of utilizing the water-power was quite ingenious, and withal simple. It consisted of a stout beam of wood, unevenly balanced upon a forked tree or post, near a running brook with a little waterfall. At one end of this beam was a great wooden "pestle," while at the end opposite was a bowl or trough, which, when empty, occupied a position exactly under the waterfall. As the bowl filled with water that end became heavier than the other, and descended slowly toward the ground, lifting into the air at the same time the opposite end of the beam, with the heavy wooden pestle attached. But at the end thus depressed, the water ran out of the trough; it became much lighter than the weighted end, which at once descended with a *thud* upon the grain. This again brought the empty trough under the little stream, and the same process was repeated. As I timed them with my watch, the number of strokes averaged four a minute. It required no attention, and in course of time would of course accomplish a fair amount of work. A rude hut was erected over the wooden bowl containing the grain, to shield it from bad weather. At various points in the mountain districts I have heard similar sounds while passing along, and once or twice have seen part of the mechanism at work, but without understanding it.

The use of water-power in the form of a wheel is also quite general along this highway. Usually the wheels are undershot; others are only used when the natural fall of water is considerable. I have frequently seen undershot wheels in a stream running through a village street; the work was slow but continual.

Returning to the inn, I passed the village temple, so crowded with people of every rank that it was evident some *fête* or other was in progress. Every one, merchants and country gentlemen, as well as labourers, had donned their best garments, and all the men of the working class had their heads newly shaven in honour of the day. The European style of dressing the hair is very rarely adopted by any except the higher classes; the coolie, the farm-labourer, adheres yet to the fashion of his forefathers. After much beating of gongs and excited clamour of expectation, a procession was formed in front of the temple to march through the town. First came a sort of miniature temple or shrine, mounted on a platform, and attached like a sedan-chair to a stout pole, by which, on the shoulders of four happy coolies, it was borne. To the pole itself were also tied two drums, or "tom-toms," which were most lustily beaten; and everything was profusely adorned with paper streamers. A little distance behind this came a sort of sacred ark, most gaudily decked out with jingling bits of brass and bronze, also carried by coolies, and ornamented in the same fashion. The bearers of this wore over their own robes peculiar gowns, doubtless belonging to the temple; and, judging from their faces, seemed to consider themselves sufficiently paid for their labour by the honours to which they were appointed. This seemed like a sort of shrine, and was regarded with great reverence. As it went by, I saw several women make the gesture of adoration by rubbing the palms of the hands softly together. Outside the temple grounds, and in the highway, a very curious and incomprehensible struggle took place between the bearers of the shrine first mentioned, those in front pushing backwards, while the two in the rear used their utmost exertions to force them along the road. What it all meant was a mystery; the crowd, however, looked happy, and the gorgeously arrayed priests fanned themselves leisurely, as if waiting for the performance of a necessary ceremony. The progress of such a procession was naturally slow. A few yards would be gained, then half of it lost by vigorous pushing backward; and, after watching it for an hour, I went back to the inn.

After sunset a great shouting was heard, and presently an immense car, two stories in height, drawn by an excited, perspiring crowd, was seen slowly progressing up the narrow street. It was brilliantly lighted by Chinese lanterns; priests were seated in each of the two stories, and although their position seemed anything but safe they fanned themselves placidly, and tried not to appear nervous. The huge thing creaked and groaned along the narrow road, knocking now and then against the roof of a house, and necessitating its readjustment in a straight road by the main force and strength of strong arms lifting the front part of the vehicle. It suggested the car of Jagenath, of which one used to read; but there was nothing solemn or awe-inspiring about it, but rather the utmost jollity and good humour. I watched it for an hour, and then went to bed amid the noisy shouts of an eager crowd, and the ceaseless clamour of fife and drum.

August 21, *Agematsu.*—Long before light I was awakened by pilgrims saying their prayers before departing on their way, some of them praying louder and longer than any previously heard. They left early, and the house was tolerably quiet for an hour or two. About ten o'clock in the forenoon others began to arrive, all hungry. When lunch or dinner is announced, they seat themselves on their heels in two long rows, facing each other, and before each man is placed a little lacquer table, or stand, about six inches high, containing his food. Everything seems devised only as a flavour to rice. A large wooden bucket is brought into the room, the cover is removed; and from the steaming contents a little maid is busily engaged filling and refilling the rice-bowls. When a Japanese enjoys his food, it is only good manners for him to express audibly his gustatory satisfaction. All pilgrims seem to have excellent appetites.

My baskets are open, and the contents scattered about. How cosmopolitan one's wardrobe becomes by much travel! Nearly all my luggage has gone on to Kobe by steamer. I have by me only necessities, and yet here, in the heart of Japan, I have with me articles bought in Leipsic, Rome, Paris, London, New

York, Omaha, Salt Lake City, San Francisco, and Yokohama!

Until three o'clock, indoors, writing; then out for a walk. A crowd surrounded a man dancing with a huge wooden mask over his head, supposed to represent some mythical beast—a lion, or bear, or perhaps a dragon; but, painted red, it had no semblance to anything living. The dragon, to cap the absurdity of the affair, personified a dancing girl, and, with a partner, went through all the languishing attitudes and evolutions in a most grotesque fashion, and yet very gracefully. Exactly what it had to do with the religious ceremonial of yesterday afternoon I cannot see, but something. These masks belong to temples; the dancers neither asked money for their performance, nor was any given them; it was "a free show." After each dance the mask was removed, and placed, by the performers, in a sort of shrine, which they carried from place to place in the village, and repeated the same performance. Attracting quite as large crowds, especially of children, was a man who did a thriving trade in modelling figures, chiefly animals. Taking in his hands a bit of some white substance resembling rice-dough, he rolled it into a chubby mass; then two snips with a pair of scissors, and two long ears were evolved; four more cuts below created as many legs. Two red eyes were added, and in a minute a little white rabbit was sitting on a bit of wood nibbling at an ear of green corn. The artist then, with a morsel of the same material, fashioned a little white saucer; red and blue ornamentations adorned the edges. It was placed on the bit of wood before the rabbit, a minute quantity of coarse brown sugar was ladled into it, two other rabbits were represented with noses in the saucer, the ears of all were gilded, and the whole affair offered for sale for two sen, or less than a penny. I fancy they were eatable, at least there was nothing deleterious about them. Bought one, and, after examination, offered it to a ragged child, but his good fortune so frightened him that only through much urging of a grandmother could he be induced to take it out of my hands.

At the upper end of the village, I noticed a path leading into rice patches in the direction of the river, and following its windings, I came at last to the riverside, some distance above the town. It was a beautiful place; the river, deep and clear, flowing at this point round the base of a huge rock projecting into the stream, and towering above it nearly fifty feet; and should any traveller resting at Agematsu desire a cool plunge in the river, I could not advise him to seek a pleasanter spot than this. The current in the centre of the stream is very swift, and one is easily swept into it, but a few good strokes will bring him again into still water. I should think that the water at the base of the rock might be ten or twelve feet deep, but it is as clear as a mountain brooklet.

After supper, while writing letters, I heard behind me the words, " Good evening, sir," and turning, found two young Japanese visitors. I invited them to take seats on the floor, offering, of course, to sit down in the same manner. " No," said one, " I shall command other chairs," which he proceeded to do. He turned out to be a young official employed in the town, and had learned a little English while attending the university at Tokio. His companion could not speak English at all; he was an ex-magistrate of the town, and seemed widely acquainted with officials in Tokio and elsewhere. Referring to a statement of Miss Bird, that suicide was very common, especially among women, he asserted, as a matter of personal observation and experience, quite the contrary; men, not women, are most given to self-destruction. In matters like this, figures and not impressions are, however, the only authorities reliable. My visitors stayed until ten o'clock, probably keeping other guests awake, and then, with much ceremony, departed.

August 22.—After breakfast the landlord rendered his bill, a yen and three-fourths (four shillings and sixpence). It was nearly double previous charges; but, then, I have enjoyed more attention and comfort, to say nothing of civility, which doubtless entered into calculations. At least twenty times during my stay here the worthy man has done me obeisance, never once without dropping on his knees and touching the floor with his forehead. Could one expect to be thus honoured for nothing ?

It was impossible, he said, for a pack-horse to carry me on, and although I could not see why, I engaged one karuma, as he suggested, and walked on to Suwara. I can convey no idea of the beauty of this road; it is well worth the journey from Tokio to one who admires natural scenery. Two miles beyond Suwara the bridge spanning a deep ravine and a mountain torrent had been carried away, and the only method of gaining the other side was by single planks, placed from boulder to boulder over the swiftly dashing current. We unloaded the karuma, and the coolie, taking his carriage on his back, led the way to the other side over this narrow bridge and then returned for my baskets. It was a curious sight, much as if one should see a horse with his cart strapped to his back as a burden. The bridge seemed to have been down some time, but there were no signs of its being rebuilt. Doubtless the question is one of money. Japan is exceedingly poor; if European nations and America had combined to ruin her financially, they could hardly have worked more certainly than they have done.

There is one instance along this road of what I call public robbery. Japan desired a telegraph between her two capitals and her two principal ports, Kioto and Tokio; Kobe and Yokohama. It runs along the Naka-sen-do, a distance of three hundred and thirty-five miles. The telegraph-posts are well planted, *but each one is supplied with a lightning rod, projecting a few inches in the air above its top, and terminating in the ground!* Now, it would be interesting to know who proposed this addition to the safety of the telegraph? Who built or set up the line? Who profited by the additional expense for an utterly absurd and useless wire? I do not know how many posts to a mile there are; if there are twenty, Japan has paid for over six thousand lightning protectors on a single line of her telegraphs which have served only one purpose, that of enriching somebody at the nation's expense. Was he a European or an American?

At Mitono we found ourselves in a town which but recently had been almost utterly destroyed by fire. Here was an excellent opportunity for widening streets and making other improvements; the inhabitants, however, were busily engaged erecting on the old foundations exact counterparts of their previous dwellings, and all available space was occupied by bamboo carpenters and mud-masons. About three o'clock I reached Tsumago, and went at once to the best inn, where, by a little diplomacy, I obtained at once excellent quarters.

The truth is, I begin to suspect my method of procedure in regard to native inns has been wrong. In the first place, failing to get what I should have brought —some sort of letter of introduction from inn to inn— I requested my Tokio landlord to translate a note which I wrote out for him, into Japanese, and therein committed a blunder. Almost the first sentence was a statement that "I do not eat Japanese food." Now,

Japanese have as great aversion to foreign cookery as we have to theirs; and as a traveller must eat something, an innkeeper would naturally anticipate his cooking-utensils would be put to foreign uses. The sentence suggested the guest as a nuisance at the start, and for the past three or four days I have not shown it. One is supplied, of course, with Japanese food which he doesn't want; but generally one or two dishes are palatable, and it is easier to order hot water for the beef-tea, in addition to their food, than to make an innkeeper understand for what purpose one can possibly wish the water alone.

Another mistake has been in applying for accommodation, and giving the innkeeper an opportunity to refuse. When one arrives late at night, this is well enough, for at that time inns are generally full, and a vacant apartment is rare. But I have made the same polite interrogatory at midday as at sundown, "Can I stay here to-night?" Here at Tsumago I first ventured on another course. Going at once to the best inn, where I knew that at this hour (3 p.m.) travellers had not begun to drop in for the night, I simply saluted the innkeeper, and, without any questions, paid off my man, and was on his hands. I confess he did not seem overjoyed at my coming, and apparently scolded the coolie for bringing me; yet they treated me well enough, and gave me a good room upstairs.

After supper the son of the landlord took me out to

see the village. We visited together the two rival temples, the Buddhist and Shinto; the two bridges across the river, and a primitive-looking schoolroom, with desks and walls bespattered with ink. My guide, by the most expressive kind of symbolic language, gave me to understand that he was the village schoolmaster; he pointed to the teacher's desk, then touched himself, and imitated the action of flogging a bad boy. Every one throughout the village was exceedingly polite to him; his schoolroom was a part of the Buddhist temple, and in some dim way they may perhaps associate his functions with those of the priest. In the evening I watched a party of chess-players in the next room. The game, in movements, is the same as ours, but the different pieces are entirely dissimilar, being all of uniform shape though varying in size. On each piece is inscribed in Chinese characters its name. The game was played without much deliberation, being more like draughts or "checkers" in one respect: there is no moving backwards.

August 23.—While packing my baskets by candle-light a little green tree-toad startled me by a leap into the room, attracted apparently by the flame. It was not very timid, and was captured without difficulty. It was, perhaps, an inch long, not larger than a grasshopper, and of a beautiful tint. Presently it gave a leap from my hand against the smooth screen, up which it walked

Mounted aloft on a pack-horse, I set out early for the Magome Pass. All this portion of the Naka-sen-do is a continuous up-and-down journey, impossible for the jinrikisha; one must either ride or go afoot, and one hill is hardly surmounted before another begins. It was early breakfast-time as we set out. In one cottage three little children were seated demurely on their heels before the mother, who was alternately feeding them with rice, each in turn. A young girl was kneeling before a shrine; somewhat beyond, the father of the family was at his devotions for the entire household; all around him, at least, other work was being done. Two bridges had been carried away, and in their place three trees had been cut down and thrown across the chasm, forming a pathway strong enough, but scarcely more than *thirty inches wide!* The horse exhibited some natural hesitation at following his leader over such a bridge with a torrent dashing amid rocks ten or fifteen feet below. It quickened its pace considerably when in the middle, as if anxious to have done with it, and I was in full sympathy with him.

Half-way up the mountain we met another pack-horse coming down, led by an old woman. The two carriers stopped, exchanged the usual compliments, but seemed to gossip more than was necessary. At last the owner of my horse approached and explained as well as he could that they proposed shifting burdens, he taking charge of the old woman's merchandise and duly delivering it in the town, turning me over to her; thus saving each of them a return journey without a load. It was manifestly so convenient an arrangement that I had no disposition to interfere, as I might have done, with a proposition which reckoned a traveller as equal to so many hundredweight of Japanese commodities. My new guide took occasion to renew the straw shoes of her steed, gossiping all the while as fast as her tongue could chatter. Finally all was arranged, and we started on our separate ways.

My conductor was a perfect specimen of the peasantry of Japan, hale, hearty, strong, nearly sixty years old; yet before eight o'clock that morning she had already walked a dozen miles. She wore a blue cotton Japanese *yakata*, or gown, with a broad sash about the waist; lower limbs encased in tight-fitting blue cloth leggings, ending at the ankle; feet bare, except straw sandals, and a large straw hat completed her attire. I could not feel comfortable, ambling along, perched on horseback, with a woman old enough to be my mother walking afoot; it seemed as though in fairness we ought to exchange places. I dare say, however, she could have given me a dozen miles' start in a walking-match, and then have beaten me; but, notwithstanding my confidence in her strength and vigour, I walked more to-day than I should have done had my guide been a man.

Nearly every day some new phase of industry among

the peasantry attracts my attention. Along the road on either side, as we descended into the valley, grass was spread out to dry; the people cut it with their little sickles wherever they find it growing on hillside or by-paths, and carry it home tied on their backs, to make hay. Water-mills of the kind described in the last chapter were quite frequent on this pass, and another kind, consisting of four square boxes arranged on the circumference of a wheel so that they were alternately emptied and filled, were also seen. The only advantage it possibly could have over a regular water-wheel, was the interrupted action necessary in a mill for pounding instead of grinding.

As the old woman drew near her home in Nakatsugawa, she appeared, I thought, anxious to have her neighbours see the new sort of business in which she was engaged; long before she came opposite their doors, she called them by name, and a crowd stood in every doorway as we went by. I found a charming little tea-house here; no other guests, so I had a large room to myself on the second floor, with nothing but green fields between the house and the distant hills. Here I took dinner and a nap, occupied the room for a couple of hours, and my bill when presented was six sen, or twopence! The place was a very pretty one; in the garden was an artificial pond stocked with trout; they were evidently kept here for customers, awaiting demand, as it was quite easy to catch one with a hand-net whenever wanted.

Before coming in I had asked my worthy and venerable guide how much she wished to take me five miles further on, to Oi, and agreeing to her terms, expected to have her company yet longer. While at dinner, however, she exchanged me for a shorter journey, and I found myself delivered over to a one-eyed, surly-looking fellow, whom I did not like at all.

The mountain passes have now been surmounted, and the road is sandy and uninteresting. The heat was very great; that and the swaying motion of the horse combined to make me exceedingly drowsy. Two or three times I found myself half unconscious, and in danger of pitching head-foremost under the horse's heels; it was only by dismounting and walking that wakefulness could be maintained. It is very curious this sensation of struggle between nature and recognized danger; I fancy it must be nearly the same as that experienced by travellers overtaken and lost in a snowstorm, whose only chance of life consists in keeping awake.

Reached Oi—a town unique in its vowel name—about three o'clock; went bravely to an inn, and found no difficulty, now that I make none by giving them the option of refusal. I sometimes think my Tokio friends might have saved me a deal of annoyance by giving a few hints in regard to the inns of the interior. But they may never have travelled much in their own country, though with wide experience of America and Europe.

A walk through the town revealed nothing interesting.

Children fled at my approach, perhaps exhibiting even more shyness than usual in the regions through which I have come. Turning a corner in the street, I came upon two or three little children playing in the stream which runs through the village; all managed to get away but one little girl, who had not noticed my approach, and her perplexed, troubled attitude, too frightened as she was to run, and yet fearful of what might next happen, was worth seeing.

August 24.—From this point karumas ply on the highway, but the demands of the men are far higher than my guide-book says should be asked; they want as much to go a mile as I expected to pay for a *ri*, or two miles and a half. To Ota, twenty-seven miles, they demand eight yen, or nearly a pound. Inquiry in the town found no one willing to take less than this rate, and I compromised finally by engaging, at four yen, two karumas for just half the distance.

It occurs to me sometimes that there is another side to this question of rapacity. What, for instance, could one say, honestly and fairly, if instead of naming his price for twenty miles' travel, my Japanese coolie should leave it to me to pay him on the principle of the golden rule—exactly as I would wish to be paid for like service? For what sum would I consider myself fairly recompensed for dragging him fifteen or twenty miles along a dusty road on a hot day? How ought one to decide the value of such work? Should it be measured by what can be got? This is simply what he is doing. By its value to me? Why, I should pay ten times the amount if I could not get away otherwise. There is a mean somewhere, but I can hardly believe my necessities the standard.

Leaving Oi about eight o'clock, found three men employed, and two vehicles. The road to Okute lay over a succession of little hills, thirteen in number—most disagreeable. The country around is bare and desolate-looking, contrasting most unfavourably with Japan as hitherto seen; hardly a dozen cottages were passed in as many miles (one village excepted), and only here and there were patches of arable land to be seen. Water-melons begin to greet the traveller at wayside refreshment houses; it is perhaps the only worthy product of this region. A little tea is grown by peasants for home consumption; near Hosokute I noticed it drying in the sun upon mats spread in front of the country cottages. The habit of taking a siesta at midday is more universal than about Tokio. At one village I passed about noon by an open door of a cottage, wherein were to be seen fast asleep every member of the family—father, mother, and one or two children. Women, especially the younger ones, almost invariably throw aside the upper portion of their robe and sleep nude to the waist. An artist would find in Japan a new world, and not in scenery only. I have seen more than one sleeping beauty that Canova would have wished as a model, and Titian have deemed not unworthy the immortality of his art.

With all its pleasures of independence, travelling alone has some drawbacks. They are insignificant, but they annoy. To-day, for instance, at Hosokute, where I lunched, I wanted a cup of tea, and from a small store I carry with me I took a pinch or two and dropped into a tea-cup, and gave to the servant. Of course I expected her to take it to the kitchen and make tea in the usual method. She simply filled the cup with hot water, and returned it with most of the tea swimming on the surface. I could not make her understand what I wanted for a long time, and then only by sending for the tea-pot and tea-kettle and making it myself. If one gets vexed or angry at such apparent stupidity it only frightens the girl who waits on you.

As the demands of my coolies increased beyond all conscience, I excused them at the end of their engagement, and, hiring a single porter to carry my luggage to Mitake, set out afoot. The afternoon was pleasant, a slight breeze mitigating the heat. Much of the way was up and down hill, and in this kind of road it hardly pays to hire a karuma; you must always walk uphill, and very often walk down. The soil is sandy, the surface denuded of verdure except in patches; even the trees in many parts are mere shrubs. At one village I saw the process of grinding meal carried on by means of a mill not unlike those one sees at Pompeii—a hollow, conical-shaped millstone revolving round and over another cone projecting into it. The peasant, his wife and daughter, side by side, trudged round and round, pushing the pole which carried the upper stone around, and slowly ground out the meal. A different style of roofing houses here obtains from what I have seen in the mountainous parts over which I have come. In many of the Naka-sen-do towns among the hills, roofs are nearly flat, and their covering of coarse shingles, surmounted by heavy pieces of rock at irregular intervals, is not very unlike what the traveller sees in some parts of Switzerland. Now the fashion of using bluish tiles begins to appear, especially in the larger towns.

In this province the images of Buddha and other gods which adorn the wayside, instead of being statues, are frequently only carved in bas-relief and painted. Often, too, they are provided with a little chapel, a stone recess in the side of the hill by the roadside. Pilgrims are fewer, yet at one place we passed the stone image of a saint or deity erected on a miniature island in an artificial pond, upon which a pious wayfarer was surprised on his knees.

I reached Mitake about three o'clock, intending to take karuma on to Ota, but as none were to be had, I put up for the night. Found no trouble in obtaining accommodation in the best inn, by simply asking no questions and giving no chance for refusal. The Japanese is intensely suspicious, and I fancy that in many cases the very act of inquiry was considered a just and reasonable ground for refusing the traveller admission.

Once admitted, however, I believe there is no other country in the world where for the same sum a traveller can have greater comfort. It is a conclusion to which I have referred before now, but succeeding experiences emphasize it the more. Once accustomed to its peculiarities, a Japanese inn of the better class is a far more agreeable stopping-place in summer time than the middle-class hotels of provincial England, Europe, or America. Take the one in which I am now writing in the village of Mitake. It is five o'clock of a summer afternoon; no other guests have arrived; the screens are all down, and a cool breeze blows from the front garden to the one in the rear, belonging exclusively to my room. Divested of dust-covered garments, I have put on Japanese costume, which on a hot day is the nearest possible realization of Sidney Smith's ideal of happiness. The little maid has brought into the room a carved brasier, with glowing charcoal in the centre; a tiny little copper tea-kettle is singing over the coals, and a lacquer tray, with tea-cups, tea-pot, and a cannister of native tea, is placed on the mat before me. The tea-pots are the most diminutive things possible, holding hardly more than half a pint. I use my own supply of tea, and offer her a cup. It is the highest of compliments, and she sips it slowly and almost reverently, looking all the while with childlike curiosity at the stranger-guest.

The end of my room next the wall is divided by a

slight partition into two recesses, one to the left being somewhat higher than the other; this is the place of honour, and where two guests occupy the same room, here sits the chief in rank. Two friends travelling together must alternately occupy this place, or one will be accounted and treated as the superior. Above this recess are sliding panels opening into tiny cupboards. I have opened these repeatedly, but never found anything stowed away. Over the windows looking towards the garden are generally wood carvings—birds and flowers, a hen and chickens, bamboo leaves, etc., always something ornamental, and executed with a fidelity worthy of an art-loving people.

As to cleanliness, the inns are incomparably superior to the "temperance houses" or inns frequented by commercial people in England. Fleas are the curse of the land in summer, but they exist as well in other countries.

On the platform which runs around the mats of an inn, one finds adjoining the garden a small wooden table, on which are two heavy copper basins. A large earthen pot near by is filled with fresh water; here one performs his ablutions. A defect certainly; one would prefer to wash face and hands in his own room, but this is a manifest impossibility where the matting upon which one treads is to be used as a bed at night. You prefer your own wash-bowl; but these are kept bright and clean. You do not fancy sleeping on the floor; but more than two hundred million subjects of the Empress of India will lie down to-night upon harder beds than the clean mats of the poorest Japanese.

Supper is brought. I have discovered that, in addition to beef-essence-soup and rice, a very palatable dish may be made of *go-zen*, or boiled rice, and "Moore's chocolate and milk." It is as easily made, needing only hot water, and forms an addition to a somewhat monotonous fare. Occasionally, however, all the dishes brought to me are at least palatable to a hungry traveller. There are usually five kinds of food served on the little lacquer stand; one dish in its centre and another in each corner, with rice of course *ad libitum*. I remove the cover from a steaming bowl, a sort of fish soup with vegetables; the addition of a little red pepper makes it very relishable. The second is a cup containing raw onions in shreds, seasoned with an acidulous approach to vinegar. The third is a peculiar sauce, of materials unknown, which is nearly always present at every repast. A dish of rice occupies the last cover, while on the plate in the centre are brook trout, fresh caught and just cooked. If there is one art in which the Japanese especially excel it is in the preparation of fresh fish for the table.

One of the coolies has just made me a ceremonious visit. After much beating of the bush, he expressed a wish to take me to Gifu to-morrow, a distance of twenty-five miles, and asks eight shillings. As he had done so well to-day, I have accepted his terms.

CHAPTER XIII.

MITAKE TO OTSU.

Across the Kisogawa—Bridge-building—Melons—Gifu and its silks—Seki-ga-hara—Akasaka—An honest friend—Samegai—Same inventions from universal needs—Lake Biwa—Steamboat to Otsu—Mi-i-dera monastery—A Japanese Samson—Ben-kei's giant soup-kettle.

August 25.—If from sound slumbers awakening must be, there is certainly no more agreeable call to consciousness than music and the soft monotone of a chant. At the first streak of dawn in this part of the country the house begins to stir, and the pilgrims, assembling together, chant softly their morning prayers. To see them thus engaged on their knees, all robed in white, is an impressive spectacle.

After breakfast paid my account of thirty sen (about tenpence) as the charge for accommodation, and was off before sunrise. Many of the villagers were already up; the women preparing the morning meal, the men sweeping the pathway in front of their cottages. The road was generally downhill, and travelling quite easy. Just before reaching Ota we came to the banks of the large river Kiso-gawa, and crossed it in a flat-bottomed ferry-boat, propelled and directed by means of a bamboo pole.

Hence for several miles the scenery was as fine as one could wish. We have left behind the mountains and the sandy hills which succeeded them, and are now following the banks of a river in a broad and fertile valley. At one point, where the road winds under a huge overhanging cliff—in fact excavated out of the rock—with the broad river flowing below, green fields and wooded hills in the distance, the view is as fine as any scene in Switzerland.

Near this point the road passes over a broad and shallow tributary of the Kisogawa, across which labourers were building a long dyke, or perhaps repairing one. Apparently great care was taken to obtain a good road bed on this dyke. After fascines of willow rods had been laid down on the rude timbers a covering of heavy stones was superimposed, and these were being covered with earth, brought from some distance in bags of hempen netting. The edges of the road were slightly raised by a double row of small stones, perhaps a foot apart; between these a layer of fresh earth, and on top newly cut sod. I thought at first that the grass and flowers I have noticed on bridges were the result of chance, instead of design; but as every process I have described was being simultaneously carried on in the construction of the long dyke, it gave me an excellent opportunity of seeing native engineering.

At Unuma, where I stopped to take lunch, the coolies intimated a desire to go on with me to-morrow, apparently somewhat anxious to be engaged before Gifu is reached. In many respects it is pleasant to have the same men with you; and offering them what I thought a fair sum to carry me to Maibara, they accepted so quickly that I feel sure they have made a good bargain.

A flat country is generally lacking in interest, except where commerce centres in towns. Mile after mile one sees almost the same objects, and meets, with but slight variations, the same incidents. Just beyond Ota I surprised a large green frog crossing the road hurriedly, like a thief anxious to escape pursuit. His booty on this occasion was a grasshopper of the same colour, which was still alive and making most vigorous but ineffectual efforts to escape his fate. It is the second time in Japan that I have seen frogs with living prey in their possession, considerably larger than I supposed they were accustomed to catch.

Melons are now cheap and abundant. In villages the housewife spreads them upon a clean board; one is cut, so that travellers may be the more tempted by a slice than they would be by the entire melon. In flavour I certainly do not detect any inferiority to those of other countries. Near Gifu I saw a cleverly contrived syphon made of sections of bamboo, jointed together at right angles, through which, from a pail near the ceiling, a continuous little fountain of water was thrown upon sliced melon below. Did the Japanese discover the principle of the syphon independently of other nations?

We reached Gifu shortly after three, and were directed at once to a good inn, so good, indeed, as to be almost worthy of a loftier designation. Unlike country hotels, this one consisted of several detached houses, connected only by covered ways, so that a visitor might, if fortune favoured, be some distance from the offices, the kitchen, or the hilarious guests. The room given me was the largest I have had in Japan; it was a little summer house by itself, and exceedingly neat.

Gifu is a large provincial town of about eleven thousand inhabitants, the capital of the prefecture. It appears to be a very prosperous city; it is certainly neat and well-ordered. Walking through the principal street, it seemed to me that I had seen no place so full of children, except Salt Lake City. I came near a pretty little child, five or six years old, before it saw me, and wishing to make its acquaintance, held toward it a penny. It was curious to watch in the child's face the conflict between desire of acquisition and fear of consequences. Could one but know the thoughts that go through the childish brain! As it made no signs of approaching me, and yet regarded me most attentively, I ventured to take a step nearer, still holding toward it the coveted coin. Immediately, however, with a little gesture of repulsion, the hand beating the air downwards, it shrieked, "Yat! yat!" and burst into a fit of crying that nothing could pacify. Evidently it thought I was about to seize it, and then what else might not happen!

In Japanese towns, foreign imports aside, nearly everything of utility is of home manufacture, and one city, therefore, in its shops at least, is almost the counterpart of another. There is but one manufacture in Gifu that I have not seen elsewhere; this is the weaving of crape, in which ordinary silk is interwoven with that produced from a certain " wild worm," or *yamamai*. The threads of silk from this latter source are much more glistening, and are not so distinctly affected by dyes as those of the ordinary species. The fabrics thus woven have a singular and beautiful appearance. I purchased some little scarfs of silk crape, upon which were either painted or inwoven little pictures—a boat at sea, or a fisherman at his nets—simple, but exquisitely done. They are of a texture so fine that I drew through a finger ring a fabric a yard wide.

The hotel rapidly filled with guests towards evening, but as the earliest arrival I had the first use of the bathroom. The girl who announced its readiness was, in costume at least, not unlike some statues one sees of Diana. For greater freedom she had slipped her gown from one shoulder and arm, leaving them entirely nude;

and yet she seemed as unconscious of any impropriety in her dress as a Greek maiden would have done two thousand years ago.

August 26.—The long day's journey of thirty miles has brought me to the banks of Lake Biwa, and from this point I shall leave the Naka-sen-do for steamboat and cars. So far as scenery is concerned, the route to-day has been monotonous; the country flat, the villages generally poor and without interest. As we approach the ancient capital, one finds more localities identified with the national history or local tradition. Here is a ferry which Yoshitomo crossed when fleeing westward after his defeat in 1159. Nearer to Kioto are the tombs of two priests, put to death about 1198 because they had persuaded Matsumushi and Suzumushi, two beautiful damsels, to leave the harem of the emperor and become nuns. Incidents trifling as these are yet matters of remembrance and record. We pass near battle-fields, scenes of as bloody and momentous events as any in Europe, yet of which contemporaneous Europe never dreamed. Fields of rice are flourishing where Kono Morono, with ten thousand men, met and defeated an army far superior in numbers in the year 1340; and just out of the village of Seki-ga-hara they point out the mound, significantly known as the "head-pile," near which, in 1600, Iye-yasu, the founder of the Tokugawa dynasty, which lasted until 1868, won a battle no less momentous in Japanese history than was

Waterloo for Europe. Here, too, is the spot where a certain barrier was erected in the year A.D. 673. One wonders in whose favour would have been the comparison if some traveller could have compared the Japan of that period with the England and Scotland of our ancestors living at the same time?

One flourishing little town, Akasaka, does a thriving trade in articles sculptured out of red, black, yellow, grey, and mixed marbles and cornelians, found in the vicinity; in fact, nearly every shop in the village is that of a lapidary. After making some purchases in one of them, I came away, forgetfully leaving behind me my guide-book with maps of the country; and I had gone probably an hour's journey before discovering the loss. The first impulse, of course, was to turn round and go back; but a moment's reflection suggested the needlessness of this, and its unknown cost in the increased demands of the two coolies. Going on, therefore, to the next village, I left the men to their pipes and gossip, engaged a fresh coolie, and started backward, a distance of perhaps five miles, with considerable doubtings whether I should ever see the book again. While in Tokio, I had taken the precaution to have my name and address written in Japanese on the fly-leaf, and there was of course some chance of its ultimate recovery. On going up to the door of the lapidary, where I thought it was left, the shopman met me with a gratified air, and at once produced the book, wrapped in paper, and duly addressed to me at Tokio, where he expected to send it by mail. Every compensation in the way of gratuity for his trouble was absolutely refused, a point in which he very little resembled the tradesman of England or the Continent.

Samegai is a rather pretty town, chiefly because of the remarkable spring which it contains. A stream of clear water gushes forth from the ground near the road, and runs through the centre of the town, the houses, indeed, being built on either side. The stream has been made to flow through an aqueduct of masonry, in which the inhabitants have for an unknown period been accustomed to throw bits of broken pottery and porcelain, giving the bottom a very clear and white appearance. Of course there is a legend attached to such a marvel as this, flowing as it does without apparent diminution the year round; but the tradition is insignificant.

At the village of Bamba we left the highway and turned into a narrow road leading toward the lake. Rice plantations occupied every available bit of ground, and as irrigation from flowing streams was impossible owing to the flatness of the country, it was carried on by means of wells. Here and there one saw a stout peasant drawing water from one of these reservoirs and pouring it into the ditch, which from his feet led into the rice patch.

The very striking resemblance between the wells of Japan and those in the country districts of the Northern

American States must occur to any traveller who has seen both countries; and the improbability of derivation one from the other suggests separate and distinct inventions. A well is one of the few things which cannot be transported, and one of the first necessities of civilized life. It seems to me one may almost trace the steps by which a common necessity in widely distant countries has led to precisely the same inventions. The village well at Ichi-no-miya, for example, is walled from the bottom with round stones, as with us; for even a savage notices that a hole in the ground will cave inwards unless this be done. Secondly, some protection is necessary to prevent accidental falling into it, and the square parapet of wooden beams precisely resembles those built about New England wells. Thirdly, one notices that rain makes the water more turbid; and the well is roofed. The simplest method of drawing water is by means of a bucket attached to a long pole. This, however, demands strength; and so, fourthly, some inventive genius attaches the bucket to a rope passing over a pulley and so balances it with a weight that a child may lift it. Finally, it is seen that instead of a dead weight balancing the water, it is better to use two buckets—the empty one descending, partly balancing the full bucket which is being raised. Now, in every one of these respects I have seen wells in Japan which coincide exactly with those common in country districts of New York and New England. Is it not reasonable to suppose that instead of one people's copying the invention of another, each originated these adaptations to their wants from the pressure of common necessities? Yet, if so, why may not other conditions of civilization have a similarly distinct origin? In the characters forming the written language of Japan there is not the slightest proof of any affinity to our own. A Buddhist monk a thousand years ago invented a kind of syllabic alphabet (if one may use the term) from the Chinese. Our characters may be traced to the Phœnician; thence probably to Egyptian hieroglyphics. Between Chinese symbols and those of the Egyptian there is as great dissimilarity as exists between either and the Mexican hieroglyphics or the rude totem of a North American savage. Even in spoken language philologists fail to connect the Chinese with the Sanscrit, from which Europe takes her dialects. True, the ages which have passed may have erased, as it were, the original likeness; but I see no reason why civilization may not have had more than one starting-point among the races of mankind. I have referred merely to one point, but the traveller in Japan will see a hundred others to which like reference might be made. The human animal, I think, is not a blind copyist; but invention is universally the necessary result of conditions demanding amelioration, and of wants which can be satisfied by human endeavour.

About sundown reached Maibara, on Lake Biwa. It

is a village of some size, and no trouble was experienced in obtaining accommodation; in fact, I took the first that I happened to see.

August 27.—Except a short "constitutional," spent the morning indoors writing, as the day is very warm. The steamboat was announced to leave at noon, and the landlord sent out and bought my ticket, including it in his reckoning, and when the hour of departure drew near sent a boy with me. The little steamboat which was to take us up Lake Biwa to Otsu, over thirty miles, was not much larger than those which ply up and down the Thames. They are constructed in Japan, sailed and managed by Japanese, who take both to steamboats and railroads immensely. The front of the boat was third class, and, of course, well filled with passengers; the aft cabin was divided into two sections, separated, however, by a partition only a foot high, forming the first and second-class compartments. The difference between them was nothing, so far as comfort or cleanliness was concerned; the division honoured as the first had carpeting instead of Japanese mats, and a high uncomfortable seat, of which during the trip I was the only occupant. Half a dozen second-class passengers were my companions, since in reality there was not the slightest seclusion possible, even had it been desired. The first two or three miles of the journey were down a river or inlet, whose banks were hidden by tall reeds. Their leaves had a peculiar drooping, as if broken halfway from the stalk, an effect one sees not infrequently in Japanese pictures. Indeed, there is much in Japanese art which out of Japan is unappreciated, simply because its fidelity to nature is not recognized. To realize how accurately they have observed and reproduced the most insignificant objects one must travel in their own land.

The lake itself is pretty. It is surrounded by hills, and from the middle of the lake I saw at one time three distinct ranges separated apparently by wide valleys. There is a look of desolation about the shores which one hardly expects in a country so thickly settled. Few villages were seen, and these far apart. In many places the shores were lined with what I imagined to be a sort of fish-trap. A tightly woven fence of bamboo and stout reeds was made at certain points to convulate inwards, in such a fashion that fish entering would not easily find the right exit, and remain, therefore, imprisoned. With plenty of water, exactly the same as the lake itself, of which these yards were only enclosed sections, there is no apparent reason why fish thus captured might not be kept and "fattened" like sheep in a pasture. At any rate, they are more easily captured whenever wanted.

We passed a large number of junks belonging to fishermen, sometimes scudding along under full canvas at a considerable rate of speed. The sail was square in shape, and had this peculiarity, that the longitudinal sections of cloth composing it were not united together;

it was in reality half a dozen sails, side by side, of the same shape and length. The boats seemed to go well enough, notwithstanding they could hardly get the full advantage of any breeze. The steamboat stopped once or twice at small towns, and reached Otsu, at the head of the lake, before sundown. Found a lad to carry my luggage, and he conducted me to an inn nearly opposite the railroad station, where I was given a room with table and chairs. I might have gone on to Kioto to-day, but preferred to see something of the place.

I walked through the town to a hill upon which is the ancient monastery of Mi-i-dera. A good climb brings one to an open plaza, in which stands a granite obelisk erected to the memory of some soldiers who lost their lives during the Satsuma rebellion of 1877. From this point an excellent view of the lake and the city of Otsu is obtained.

A small boy, easily tempted by some coins from the errand upon which I fear he had been sent, conducted me through the wood to the site of the old monastery. It was founded A.D. 675, but none of the original buildings probably remain. Pilgrims were going from place to place, regarding with special veneration several objects which remind one of the relics shown at the porter's lodge of Warwick Castle. There is an immense bell, no doubt more than a thousand years old, about which inventive fancy has created a legend, resembling the story of Samson and the gates of Gaza. One of the retainers of Yoshitune, Ben-kei by name, noted for his great strength, is said to have stolen this bell, and carried or dragged it to the top of a neighbouring mountain, where he amused himself in beating it, to the great discomfort of its former owners, the monks. They besought him to return it; and he finally agreed on condition that they should brew him as much miso soup as he wanted. The iron boiler used on this occasion is carefully preserved to this day; it measures at least five feet across the top. On a separate platform is the bell-tower in which hangs the veritable bell. Sceptics no doubt sneer at the legend as puerile; but the pious pilgrim points out to you in the smooth bronze of the bell itself deep scratches and indentations, which certainly seem to have been caused by rudely dragging it over rocky ground. And then there is the soup-kettle, and "uninterrupted tradition." So the satisfied countryman sibilantly murmurs his appreciation and faith; and buys rude woodcuts of Ben-kei carrying off the bell. Whether he is canonized or not, I don't know; but the country people greatly venerate any action extraordinary in itself, without too close inquiry into its ethics. Is it not so universally? Some of Samson's exploits will hardly stand the tests of a rigid morality.

CHAPTER XIV.

KIOTO.

The ancient capital—Resemblance to Philadelphia—Deified statesmen—Temples—Nan-zen-ji monastery—The thousand images of Kwannon—The great bell—Cyclopian masonry—Temple of Kiyomidzu-dera—The sin-cleansing fountain—Nude sinners —Young Japan.

Kioto, August 28.—Arrived this morning about eleven o'clock by train, and engaging a karuma by the hour, set out to discover a good Japanese inn.

There are at least two hotels kept by Japanese "after foreign style," but I desire while in Japan to patronize only native establishments. At one or two mentioned by Satow they seemed either full of guests or unwilling to take foreigners, but very civilly directed me to one where better fortune awaited me. The entrance to it was by a very narrow lane leading out of Kiya-Machi street; clean enough, but not otherwise inviting. Received by the hostess with due formalities, I made known my wants in respect to rooms. Could I stay here for a few days? She motioned me upstairs, where I found two chambers, overlooking the river Kamogawa, which at this season is little more than a narrow stream meandering through a wide pebbled-lined bed. Everything was so neat and clean, and the view from the window so charming, that I at once decided to seek no further, and established my quarters forthwith in the "Hi-rang-i-take" inn.

The uniform regularity of the streets in Kioto must attract the notice of every traveller. It is almost the exact counterpart of Philadelphia, and the coincidences between it and the city founded by William Penn are noteworthy. In both, the streets run back from a river, and at right angles are intersected by other avenues. Like Philadelphia, it is a city built by design, and the plan upon which Kioto was originally laid out has not changed during the eleven hundred years of its existence as a capital. In both cities many of the streets are designated by numerals; "First Street," "Second Street," and so forth, were laid down by a Japanese city-builder nearly a thousand years before their American counterparts were founded. Finally, to complete the comparison with the "City of Brotherly Love," the original name of Kioto, chosen by its royal founder to designate his new capital, was "The City of Peace."

I have noticed that when a great city springs from insignificant or unknown beginnings, enlarging slowly

Kioto. 173

and by the accretion of centuries, its plan is always unsymmetrical, and the streets tortuous and labyrinthine; but when, on the other hand, it is the result of a single brain, which foresees growth and enlargement, the plan is generally geometrical, and the streets often run at right angles. Examples of this first class are seen in London and Rome, Canton in China, Benares in India, Boston in America, and in a thousand other smaller towns; while most large American cities of the present century supply instances of the second statement. The capital of Mormondom, Salt Lake City, founded by Brigham Young, is as rectangular as Kioto and Ozaka, or Philadelphia and San Francisco. New York combines both peculiarities; up to fifty years ago its streets were as crooked as those of London; but as soon as its rapid development made large plans necessary, it ceased to be irregular, and in its subsequent expansion imitated Philadelphia. Of course no one could predict rectangularity of streets as a universal result of the circumstances which principally conduced to its adoption in the cities named; a city thus planned, however convenient, can hardly be called picturesque. Still, it is singular to find so many examples of the same taste among people widely separated by distance, and distinct in civilization.

I visited this afternoon a temple called Kitano Ten-jin, in the north-east suburb of the city, dedicated to a Japanese statesman, Sugawara Michizane, who flourished exactly a thousand years ago. His story strikingly illustrates the tendency of the Japanese to make demigods of badly treated heroes. A precocious youth, he is said to have become not only great as adviser to the mikado, but the best Chinese scholar Japan has ever produced, and his poetical and prose compositions in both

A BUDDHIST TEMPLE, KIOTO.

languages have earned for him equal celebrity. But falling under the displeasure of the emperor, and the envy of his less-honoured advisers, he was banished from court, and died in exile about the year 903. As with Sogoro, the wicked adviser of the emperor was troubled by the statesman's ghost, who appears also to have disturbed the conscience of the mikado himself, for he revoked, twenty years after the exile's death, his decree of banishment, and reappointed the dead man to his former high position. The present temple was founded only forty-five years after his death; he is honoured as the god of caligraphy or good penmanship. Why bronze and stone statues of reclining bulls should be specially found in his temple I can't say—probably no one knows to-day—but very good specimens are scattered about the grounds. The temple, although large, and bearing signs of former popularity, was to-day quite deserted; and I care very little for temples when the faith has gone, unless their architecture be more pleasing than those of Japan.

After sundown, the house filled with guests; the place seems, however, more of a restaurant than an inn for travellers. Adjoining it on either side are similar establishments, all facing the river. Over the water are platforms erected upon piles, and by little bridges connected with the houses; these are particularly coveted by guests as supper-rooms. Along the river as far as I can see are merry parties of young men and maidens, eating, drinking *saké*, and playing the guitar. The Japanese are as noisy as the Irish when they meet to enjoy themselves socially.

At the post-office to-day made the acquaintance of a young man who spoke very good English, learned entirely at school. It is indeed pleasant to hear one's native tongue again. He was quite obliging, and has offered to act as interpreter if I have any need of one.

August 29.—Shortly after breakfast began the day's sight-seeing by crossing the Third Street bridge, and following the road till it led into the country. My plan was to find a certain monastery on the hillside, but my map being somewhat indefinite I walked beyond it, and found myself at the gate of a nameless little Buddhist temple in the outskirts of the city. At the entrance stood the shrine of some fierce deity, before whose statue were fresh-plucked flowers in bamboo holders, evidence of pious interest, if not affection. While looking about, a young priest appeared at the door and courteously invited me into his matted parlour, ordering the servant at the same time to bring a fan and a glass of sugar and water. He inquired my name, nationality, and plans. On learning of my journey over the Naka-sen-do he seemed to consider it quite an undertaking, especially as he had never been so far away from home as Tokio. He insisted on accompanying me some distance down the road, and at parting shook hands with me; an indication that he knew something of European ways and manners.

Kioto lies in a broad valley, and principally on the west bank of the rivulet Kamogawa. The eastern suburb on the other bank of the stream terminates in hills of no great elevation, the sides of which are occupied by temples and monasteries and the groves which surround them. Nearly all the temples I have seen to-day are better preserved and more beautiful than those at Tokio; but on the other hand, with one exception, they were less frequented. An interesting temple is a part of the Nan-zen-ji monastery. It stands in spacious grounds, surrounded by trees, but has a look of desolation about it. Two young boys, in priests' garments and with shaven heads, were the guardians of the sanctuary; they permitted everything to be inspected, and even invited me upon the high altar. On either side of it are two large bronze bowls, the metal perhaps an inch thick, which are used as gongs, by striking them on the outer rim; the sound given out was remarkably clear and resonant. This temple is about six hundred years old; it has a stone floor or pavement, the only one I have seen in Japan.

Further to the south I visited a curious structure, the San-jiu-san-gen Do, a building nearly four hundred feet long, built in 1266, to receive a thousand images of the thousand-handed Kwannon, the goddess of mercy. Peering through the barred doors (one is not allowed to enter), we see an army of images, each five feet high, arranged in ten tiers gradually sloping upward, as if they were sitting in an amphitheatre. The central statue is much the largest and best, being eighteen feet high, but all are good specimens of wood carving. Of course they have not a thousand hands; the artists seem to be satisfied with half a dozen on either side; but it is said that no two statues are precisely alike in the arrangement of hands or articles in them. There is a story about the central statue; it is said to contain a human skull in its wooden head. Some centuries ago one of the mikados was troubled with a headache which no physician could heal. Finally he made a pilgrimage, at the end of which he had a dream. A spectral form appeared to him in a vision and informed his majesty that he had lived in a previous state of existence on earth—a matter of fact which the emperor had never doubted. He had been, the spectre continued, a pious and benevolent monk, whose virtues had earned for him a reappearance on earth as a mikado of Japan. In some unfortunate way, however, not explained, his former skull had not been dissolved, but from it grew a willow tree, which, whenever the wind blew, shook and caused his majesty's present head to ache in sympathy. Of course, when the mikado awoke, his first step was to find his old skull, and when once in his possession it was placed, where it was not likely to be disturbed, in the head of the chief statue of the goddess Kwannon. Is it there now? Perhaps some prying Japanese archæologist of the twentieth century will be able to tell us.

Close by this temple is another large structure, erected over a huge wooden image of Buddha, set up here at the beginning of the present century where various predecessors have been destroyed. Near it is a bell, one of the largest in Japan, fourteen feet high, nine feet in diameter, and a weight of over sixty-three tons, dimensions rarely exceeded even in the largest bells of

THE GREAT BELL.

Europe. Why does not some enterprising millionaire or citizen of the land of dollars offer to buy it? Perhaps the authorities would refuse to part with it for any sum; but nowadays Japan is very poor and might be tempted to part with so great a curiosity at a good price. Better still, I think, would be an offer to loan it, say, for fifty or a hundred years, to be returned on honour. Japan could certainly trust any nation upon such condition, to keep her art treasures for more prosperous days, even where she might not wish to part with them outright. The day will come, I hope, when all the monuments of Assyrian, Egyptian, and Grecian art, now in other countries, shall be restored to the sites from which they have been despoiled; but only when these lands shall have become prosperous and well-governed; in an age when travel shall be so cheap as to be the common privilege of students of history or art.

The grounds of this temple are surrounded by a wall worth mentioning, on account of the colossal size of the stones composing it. It is formed of a row of boulders averaging, I should think, ten feet in height; standing by them I could, with an umbrella, but just reach to the top. Between these stones the interstices are filled up with masonry. The labour of placing these vast monoliths in position with the rude appliances of former times must have resembled that of building the pyramids, or at least of laying their foundations.

By far the most interesting temple I have yet seen

was one to which I found my way after dinner, Kiyomidzu-dera. It lies somewhat further up the hillside than the majority of temples on this slope, and seems far more patronized by devotees. The streets leading to it are occupied for the most part by pottery dealers, and as you draw nearer to the grounds, a few beggars are noticeable, chiefly from their rarity everywhere else. Along the way bundles of iron "cash" are sold for a penny; they are very rusty and doubtless worthless except to be used over and over in placing before outdoor shrines.

The view of the city from this temple is very fine. Each house has its garden; one sees green foliage everywhere breaking the monotony of dull grey roofs and brown houses. Few remarkable or exceptionally high buildings are to be seen; its appearance is rather that of a city of homes; of a people whose prosperity is nearly equally shared. Was it greatly different three hundred years ago, when perhaps from this very point St. Francis de Xavier, the apostle of Christianity in Japan, looked down on the great city? He says in one of his letters that it contained ninety thousand houses, which would give a population nearly twice as great as it can claim to-day.

The origin of this temple antedates the period of authentic annals. Many centuries ago a young monk having dreamed of a golden stream flowing down this hillside, went in search of it. Ascending a brook to its source in this ravine he found a venerable old man seated by a cascade. "For two hundred years I have been here, repeating invocations and waiting for you; take my place that I may go on a journey which I must make. This is a suitable spot for a hermitage, and the log lying here will afford material for an image of the Most Compassionate One." So the young man sat down, undeterred by an example that would seem to promise a rather monotonous life. The old man did not come back; and following his track up the mountain-side, the monk found on its highest peak a pair of shoes. This convinced him (in those good old times people were more easily convinced of anything than to-day) that the mysterious stranger was none other than the goddess of mercy, Kwannon herself, who had gone up to heaven from that spot. He returned to the cascade, and there lived trying to carve an image of the Divine being. How, after many years of toil, the good monk finished his work; how he succeeded in inducing a hunter to tear down his house and to re-erect it by this cascade as a rude temple for the completed image of the goddess, these are matters beyond reasonable question. Ever since it has been a sacred place. In times of civil war it was spared; contending chiefs refrained from encroaching on its revenues or molesting its monks. The efficacy of prayers by its devotees to Kwannon became an established fact. Among the manuscripts still sacredly preserved is a letter from

Kioto.

Hidetsugu, offering to the abbot an endowment of ten thousand koku of rice (nearly fifty thousand bushels), if by his prayers he succeeded in prolonging the life of his adopted mother, "if not for three years or two years, at least for thirty days." It was a difficult task, for the aged woman was very sick; nevertheless, the abbot exerted himself so well that she did not die until three years afterward.

The cascade by which the goddess appeared has been transformed into a fountain for the ablutions of pilgrims. Three stone gutters, slightly projecting beyond the edge of the rock over which the stream once fell, conduct the water into as many currents and cause it to fall into a square stone basin, ten or twelve feet below. Directly under each stream is a small square block of stone, perhaps eighteen inches in diameter; upon these pilgrims stand and repeat their prayers, the act being meritorious in proportion to the time which the devotee can endure the water dashing over head and body. Here I saw a spectacle privileged, I fancy, to few travellers in Japan. Looking down a long flight of stone steps leading from the platform connecting the two temple buildings, I saw a number of nude figures bathing under this cascade. Descending the steps, I found half a dozen pilgrims undergoing the ceremony described, and among them three or four girls eighteen or twenty years old—all of them quite nude, with the exception of a single cloth around the loins. The young women were actual types of beauty, and not simply in features; their forms were as nature ordained, as art cares only to represent, undistorted by modern European fashions; and the sight of these living statues, with water streaming over them, against the background of dark rocks and green ferns and foliage of trees, was certainly, from an artistic point of view, exceedingly picturesque. The presence of a stranger did not disturb them, if indeed they noticed me. By turns they stepped lightly upon a block of stone under one or the other waterfall; the long hair, loosened, was streaming down the back; the head was bowed; the hands clasped in attitude of prayer; the lips murmured the invocation; until suddenly, unable to endure the penance longer, the light form sprang from beyond the reach of the cascade with a merry laugh, and another took her place. They seemed all as unconscious of impropriety as so many water nymphs —in the fairy days before nymphs left this degenerate world—taking such innocence with them. What a picture a French artist—Bouguereau, for instance—might paint: "Devotees bathing under the Sacred Fountain of Kiyumidzu-dera, Kioto, Japan." It would carry off the honours of the Salon.

Mr. Yanagishima called on me this evening, and I find him an exceedingly well-informed young man. His great desire is for opportunity to study foreign literature and history; he evidently read much while at school, but now the purchase of European books is quite beyond his means. For such young men, scattered as they are throughout the empire, the flower of "Young Japan," the best hope of her future, I feel the keenest sympathy. Their education simply awakens tastes whose gratification is beyond their reach. They master the difficulties of our language while at school, but all the culture to which it leads is denied the great majority of them, simply because our books and journals and reviews are far too expensive for their private means. And the worst reflection is that the fault is largely our own. If Japan is poor to-day, it is partly because Christian nations—England, America and others—have robbed her without scruple and plundered her without remorse; because we hold to-day in our national treasuries gold dishonestly and unjustly exacted from her in the hour of her peril and distress; because our statesmen continue—by exacting permanence in treaties of which Shylock would have been ashamed—to force her towards national bankruptcy that our factories may crush her industries, our commerce flourish, and our interests thrive at her expense.

CHAPTER XV.

THE CITY OF PEACE.

The mikado's palace — City hospital — Shimo-gamo temple — A freak of nature — Odd ceremonies — Temple of Nishi-hongwan-ji — Buddhist prayer-meeting — A youthful abbot — Chion-in monastery — Relics of antiquity — A manuscript fifteen centuries old — Musical floor — Stone Age in Japan — Kioto by night.

Kioto, August 30.—After dinner took karuma and drove to the castle of Ni-jo, now occupied by the city prefecture, to obtain permission for visiting the mikado's palace. The old building, erected nearly three hundred years ago by the great conqueror Iye-yasu, is now given over to a crowd of officials and clerks, who are continually laughing or talking or calculating aloud, in what Western people would think a most unbusinesslike fashion. With the palace of the mikado, which was next visited, it singularly contrasts. One is a castle, suited probably for a military chieftain of that period and country; the other is a plain country residence, pretty in some of its details, but the furthest removed from one's conceptions of a palace. Fancy unpainted buildings thatched with straw or bark, and furnished only with finely woven matting, designated as parts of a palace! And in simplicity like this, the emperors of Japan for a thousand years dreamed away their lives. The buildings are all modern, built in 1854, but the site has been unchanged since Kioto was founded. The palace has been burnt and rebuilt no less than six times since the beginning of the seventeenth century.

One is admitted to-day into every part of the structure, and into rooms where a few years ago it was probably death to have entered. The ordinary living room of his Majesty was a central compartment, surrounded by ante-rooms occupied by female attendants; those who had business with the mikado stated it to women, who conveyed the errand to the Son of Heaven and brought back his reply. One house is divided into tiny little rooms, such as would please children and girls. Where is the magnificence that we associate with royalty? It does not appear to have existed, according to our notions at least. The matting is of finer quality, the screens which divide the apartments one from the other are of silk and exquisitely painted with various pictures, but there is nothing to suggest extraordinary wealth or unlimited power. I do not believe there is a building on the palace grounds which if burnt to-morrow could not be duplicated for two thousand pounds. In one sense it was a prison; for it shut the emperor within, no less securely than it kept common people without. Those astute rulers who in reality governed Japan said that the surest way of making the throne secure, was to elevate its occupant to an equality with the gods and to hide him from profane eyes. How well they succeeded is shown by the fact that the present ruling dynasty in Japan is the oldest on earth.

To the city hospital, which is under charge of a German physician. He was not in when I called, but his chief assistant, who spoke German quite fluently, showed me through the building. It is beautifully situated and in most excellent order. The only case of special interest was that of a leper, whose disease, however, was in the earliest stages. Why they were keeping him as an in-patient I cannot understand, as the disease is quite incurable.

Visited next the Shinto temple of Shimo-gamo just outside the town. It was founded some twelve hundred years ago, but the buildings seemed newly painted. There were very few worshippers or even idlers standing about, and the place, like most Shinto temples, was very dreary and desolate looking. A very fine grove of trees surrounds the grounds. Near the gate are two tall trees about the same height, which are curiously connected by a branch growing from one into the heart of the other, six or eight feet distant. They are regarded

The City of Peace. 189

with great veneration; twisted straw symbols are fastened from trunk to trunk; and they are particularly visited —for what reason it is easy to see—by women who desire to live in harmony with their husbands. I confess to being a little suspicious of these "sacred trees" which so unaccountably spring up in the region of temples or shrines, some of which I have before mentioned. It is quite probable, I think, considering the Japanese knowledge of what shape trees may be made to take, that they are all the result of intention and design, rather than accident.

Returning home, found an old Japanese friend, Mr. Yangimoto, awaiting me, having come up from Kobe by train on hearing of my arrival in Kioto, to see how I was situated. We had hardly exchanged greetings and inquiries, when another young Japanese whom I met at the prefecture was announced, and we spent the evening talking of old times, and discussing, very guardedly, Japanese politics and foreign relations.

Wednesday, August 31.—I spent the greater part of the day in company with Mr. Yanagishima, who offered to act as interpreter if I wished to make any purchases.

It is a curious fact that the introduction of foreign manners in association with Europeans is not permitted to modify or supplant the ancient forms of national etiquette when Japanese associate with each other. A Japanese friend, for instance, greets me or makes his departure precisely as a European gentleman would do, with the quiet and simple formalities of ordinary civility; but it is a very different affair when he chances to meet an acquaintance or friend of his own people; even if the person encountered be equally well versed in Western methods of courtesy. When Mr. Kitasato called last night, after shaking hands with me he turned toward Yangimota, and recognized him as an acquaintance. "I know this gentleman," said Mr. Yangimota, and then rising, both young men went through that long series of formal and profound bows, interspersed with polite expressions, which make up the necessary ceremony of greeting between friends. Later, when it became time to depart, we were all seated on the floor, and both of these gentlemen in saluting each other brought their foreheads repeatedly to the floor, amid a profusion of what I suppose were the most complimentary phrases imaginable. A moment later, both of them, standing, shook hands with me and bowed exactly as Europeans would have done. I fancy it is not so much a preference for their own ceremonies, as the difficulty one experiences in omitting them without offence; the least abridgment might be inferred as a personal slight. Somebody must make a beginning, however, at no distant day, for with telegraphs and railroads and other foreign peculiarities, Japan will find her present formalities too many and too tiresome for the new life she has begun to live.

September 1.—Went this afternoon to the temple of Nishi Hon-gwan-ji, the head-quarters of one of the principal Buddhist sects. It is about three centuries old, but the sect to which it belongs took its origin in the teachings of a certain monk who lived in the thirteenth century. As in Christendom, the differences between Buddhist sects are often almost indistinguishable to foreigners, who take no interest in them; and are based frequently upon slight divergence in the interpretation of Buddhist scriptures. This Hon-gwan-ji sect, for example, maintains the possibility of salvation to all men who sincerely desire it, and that the way thereto is by faith rather than works or vain repetition of prayers. One may almost find in the Buddhist monk of the thirteenth century a prototype of the German priest of two hundred years later.

The interior of the buildings is magnificently decorated after Japanese ideas of art. The floors are covered with *tatami*, or Japanese matting, and every worshipper, of course, removes his sandals or shoes before entering. Carved cornices and richly painted screens, with winter scenery, flowers and birds, are the chief methods of decoration. It is quite impossible to describe the richness of the shrine or to make, without photographs, their shape intelligible.

Shortly after entering one of the buildings, I saw a crowd of people making their way along covered corridors toward another temple, and joining with them, I followed. The audience-room reached, each worshipper placed his shoes, or rather wooden sandals, outside, and took his position on the floor within. A peculiar hush was evident as a preliminary to some ceremony more than ordinarily solemn. Presently the doors opened and a procession of priests entered from the rear, advanced into the room and ranged themselves on either side, facing a low platform. The room was crowded, the expectancy evidently great. Suddenly and silently, a small sliding screen behind the platform opened, and a man in the gorgeous, red silken garments of a high priest entered quietly and sat down facing the audience. The excitement was intense. People stood up the better to see him, while cries from scandalized officials implored them to resume their seats. Japanese are quick to obey authority, and in a moment or two perfect order was again restored. Only murmured prayers were to be heard—the invocation to Buddha, "Nam-mu ami Dabuts"—and the soft rubbing of the rosaries. Offerings of money were freely made in the most singular fashion of tossing the money among worshippers seated in front, to be picked up subsequently by attendants. Evidently it was deemed impossible for any Japanese to appropriate such contributions, even if they fell in his lap. I saw several heads hit by coins; but their owners paid no attention, and probably hit others in front of themselves. After looking at the audience silently for about ten minutes, the High Priest arose from the floor and quickly disappeared as he came. It was doubtless only reverence that was paid

A WINTER COSTUME.

him, but I have never seen anything which seemed so closely to approach the worship of a human being.

Adjoining the grounds of the temple and belonging to it is a summer-house which once belonged to Hideyoshi, who flourished some centuries ago. It was presented to the monastery and removed to their grounds, just as I believe it was once proposed by an enterprising American to buy Shakespeare's birthplace, then a butcher's shop, and remove it to the United States. It may possess special reverence for the Japanese, but has little for us, except as the best illustration of the architectural taste of its period, which has hardly changed for centuries. The guide points out an old steam bath which Hideyoshi is said to have used, with exactly the same reverence English and Americans would give to the table upon which *Hamlet* was written, if such an article really existed. He led me into the gardens, very prettily laid out with meandering rivulets and fancy bridges of stone, rockwork, and fish-ponds. From one clear spring he wished me to drink, as the best and coolest water in Kioto, but as he waded in with bare legs to reach the spot where it bubbled up, I begged to decline.

September 2.—Seldom, in travelling about the world, have I had more pleasant quarters than here in Kioto. Nearly all the temples on the eastern slope of the hills opposite may be seen amid the foliage of trees surrounding them. In front is the almost dry bed of the river, in the pools of which fisher-boys paddle about in early morning for crabs, and picturesque groups of women are during the day engaged in the occupation of washing linen, or rather bleaching it in the sun. Ni-jo bridge offers almost as unceasing and novel a panorama as its great rival in London. Looking from my window the other evening, my friend, Mr. Yangimoto, called my attention to a group of buildings on the hillside. "There is the monastery of which Mr. Azuma was the chief priest before going abroad." Some years ago I met in America a young Japanese, who, it was rumoured, was of near relationship to the mikado, and who had come abroad of his own will to study the customs and civilization of Western nations. Unfortunately of weak constitution, he contracted consumption, and died shortly after his return to Japan.

Mr. Kitasato, from the prefecture, called again this evening. In accordance with a request from my friend, he had procured from the city authorities a letter introducing me to the present chief priest of the Chi-on-In, suggesting the exhibition of various ancient documents not often exhibited; and he will accompany me there to-morrow.

I noticed early in the evening the side of a distant mountain, Hi-yei-san, brilliantly lighted by a row of bonfires extending from base to summit. On calling Mr. Kitasato's attention to it, he said it was of the nature of a religious ceremony. "When it has been a long time without rain, as during the past summer, the peasants' rice-fields suffered for want of water. Then they go to this mountain, which is sacred, and light bonfires and pray to the gods for rain. It is what you call superstition. I do not believe in it. What good to pray to the gods? The rain comes, anyway, after a time. Then the peasants think the gods heard their prayers," he added, laughing. The young man represents very accurately the attitude of many intellectual young Japanese whom I have met. They regard with supreme contempt the religion of their fathers, nor is it that form of Christian belief which prays for rain in time of drought which is supplanting the creeds they have left.

September 3.—With Mr. Kitasato, who called shortly after noon, I visited one of the largest and most important of the Japanese monasteries, Chi-on-in. It was founded in 1211 by a Buddhist saint, known as En-ko Dai-shi, who was then seventy-eight years old. It is said that various portents accompanied his birth; but these seem never to have been wanting to any one who subsequently became noted for learning or piety in this country. One pretty story is told of him which may be true, although it also has a parallel in religious history. In his native province he became at an early age so distinguished for learning that his teacher sent him, when scarcely fourteen years old, to the great monastery of Hi-yei-san, with a letter containing merely these words, "I send you an image of the great sage,

The City of Peace. 197

Mon-ju." Naturally enough, the priest to whom it was addressed asked for the image, and was greatly surprised when the child-bearer of the message was brought into his presence. Devoting himself to the study of theology, he developed, as we should have expected, a new path to salvation; founded this monastery, and here died six and a half centuries ago, in the odour of sanctity.

A broad avenue between terraced walls of masonry and banks covered with trees, leads us to the principal entrance. On presenting the letter, it was received with a profound reverence, and we were shown into a sort of half-modernized reception-room, with carved table and heavy chairs. A gorgeously dressed priest soon entered, and we all bowed again and again. He spoke for some moments with Mr. Kitasato, who then explained to me that the chief priest or abbot to whom the letter was sent was off on a journey, but that this priest, being next in rank, was able and would be happy to display the treasures we had come to see.

The priest excused himself for a time, and during his absence a youthful monk served us with tea and confections. There were three kinds, at least in colour, for the taste was similar and the substance about the same. The nearest approach to it which I can imagine would be parched corn, ground coarsely, sweetened, coloured red, white, or blue, and then moulded into various shapes. The white confection was in shape of small *pâtés*, each stamped with the flower crest of the monastery; the red ones were like huge wafers four inches in diameter and almost as thin as paper, while the blue confection were most curiously shaped, so as to resemble leaves of grass. In taste no difference, as I have said, could be noticed.

Soon the priest made his appearance again, accompanied by four or five monks carrying wooden boxes, plain or lacquered, in which were the documents I had come to see. To me they were of interest on account of their antiquity, and the veneration they excited in others; yet after all I regarded them much as a Chinese scholar, imperfectly acquainted with Western history or religion, would survey the manuscript treasures of the British Museum or the National Library in Paris. It was far otherwise with the priests. How slowly and solemnly they opened the boxes in which these manuscripts were kept! How reverently they touched the pages upon which generation after generation had looked with perhaps equal reverence! Here, for example, is a manuscript just a little tasted by the book-worm, the characters traced in gold upon a blue or blue-purple paper; it was written a thousand years ago by a Chinese emperor. Another yet rarer manuscript was in characters of gold upon red paper, and in this respect it is unique; a date of fifteen hundred years ago is given as the time in which it is composed. Still another, partly pasted into a book the better to preserve it, was assigned to the great Ko-bo Dai-shi, hermit, priest, and

The City of Peace. 199

saint. How little significance has this name for us Europeans! And yet to Japan he is almost what St. Patrick is to Ireland, or St. Augustine to the Catholic world. I saw only a paper covered with Chinese characters, which was in existence before Alfred sat on the throne of England or Charlemagne ruled half of Europe. One design represented a Chinese pagoda of many stories, with every architectural detail complete; yet the whole was made up of written Chinese characters descriptive of the attitudes of the gods; and by beginning at a certain point near the base, one would read a continuous history, until the end was reached at a point adjoining the commencement. Most of the pictures were Chinese wall-paintings, representing incidents in the lives of saints and perils they had escaped through interposition of some deity. A very interesting portrait of Buddha, said to be more than a thousand years old, represented him rather more like the native of Hindustan which he was, than with the Chinese or Japanese features which are often unconsciously given him here. It was painted on a golden background, and the halo about the head was quite such as one sees in the paintings of the pre-Raphaelite schools, especially of Fra Angelico (1387-1455). Another picture was supposed to represent the "Five Hundred Rakan," or disciples of the master; it was painted about eight centuries ago in China, which country I was told possesses no such treasures of her own antique art, as, brought centuries ago to Japan, have been here carefully preserved.

A few curiosities of archæological interest were shown. A bottle, claimed to be of the oldest pattern known in Japan, was exhibited; the shape was more like a hatchet than a flask. Stone axes and flint arrow-heads, quite resembling those in use by the American Indians, were shown, and I was allowed to take a sketch of them. An ornament resembling tigers or bears' claws, but made of polished stone, was a very common specimen; they were pierced, and perhaps worn around the neck as symbols of authority or power. When I told the priest, through Kitasato, that the custom of wearing a necklace composed of the claws of grizzly bears was frequent among certain American tribes, he was much interested, and said that precisely the same fashion obtained among the Ainos of Yesso in Northern Japan. It seems to me by no means improbable that these Ainos are in part ancestors of the American Indians. If an intelligent Aino boy could be well educated by some missionary society, and then sent for mission-work to the coast of Alaska and British Columbia, he might possibly discover analogies of language which would be of immense interest.

The principal building of this monastery is the largest of its kind in Kioto, and perhaps in Japan, being nearly a hundred feet high. The shrine of its founder, En-ko Dai-shi, stands on a stage or altar; four gilded pillars are at each corner. I was shown through the Ho-jo, or official residence of the abbot; the screens were decorated with paintings chiefly of the seventeenth century, though an excellent painting of geese upon wooden doors is ascribed to an artist who died over three hundred years ago. The long hall-way within the building, connecting the different rooms, creaks under one's feet in a peculiarly musical fashion. I ascribed it to age, but was told it was the result of design—perhaps to prevent unanticipated intrusions. On one screen is pointed out a space through which a sparrow once flew, so naturally painted were the branches and leaves. It is an old story this, with many counterparts; they tell you in Seville of Murillo's St. Anthony that the birds sometimes fly at the vase of flowers which stands by the figure of the saint.

Buddhist priests are all shaven and shorn, and wear robes quite different from those of ordinary men. The one acting on this occasion as the chief entertainer was dressed entirely in silk; the outer robe was of a bright violet hue, very thin, and worn over a white under dress —a very brilliant man.

September 4.—I have spent the day principally in going about the streets, making little purchases, and studying the people, a pursuit to me always novel and delightful. There is one street which at night is peculiarly attractive to great crowds of both sizes, perhaps on account of the theatres. It is the fashion

A JAPANESE THEATRE.

for the manager to permit glimpses of the magnificent attractions within to be visible without during the first few minutes of the play; if a man's interest is excited he will pay the few sen necessary to satisfy curiosity. Water-melon shops on this street do a thriving trade; the guest is furnished with a bench, a plate, and a knife, three suggestive implements of another civilization. For all these, and as much water-melon as the guest can eat, he is asked a penny.

Here, too, are several photographers. This is an art which has become very popular in Japan; few villages of any size are without their "true-picture man." The attitudes taken by the fair portrait-seekers are sometimes very odd. Nearly every photographer keeps, as a part of his stock-in-trade, two or three cast-off European dresses, hats, and other articles of female apparel, and it is quite the fashion for a pretty Japanese girl to make herself a horrid "guy" with the out-worn fashions of a dozen years ago. There is just one reason why one can forgive her—she leaves her lips unpainted, and in the finished photograph they appear natural instead of black.

The street is almost as animated a scene—minus the brutality—as the Whitechapel of London or the Bowery of New York on a Saturday night. The pavement is lined with curiosity dealers in a small way; each spreads his little stock on a mat, lights a lantern or so, and awaits customers. The great majority of his articles are connected in some way with the habit of smoking, and for the most part are second-hand. Here and there are a few relics of a past feudal system—old swords, a dagger or two, or the ornaments that once were attached to them and are now separated. It is certainly remarkable into how many distinct and salable parts a Japanese weapon may be separated; frequently the sword thus disintegrated brings a better price than if left complete, especially when some portions are in poor order. The blade, for instance, has a value of its own dependent upon the quality of the steel. The pin which secures the handle is an ornament of itself. The hilt is of bronze or iron, but often inlaid with silver so as to form a small picture in bas-relief, and so hilts command a distinct market. Within the silken handle are silver and bronze ornaments, to get at which the partly worn handle is often destroyed. A small dagger often accompanies the wooden sheath; this has a separate value. Finally, this last-named article can be purchased in any quantity, displaying every degree of workmanship. Taken as a whole, I do not believe that this weapon in any European country a century ago could compare for artistic merit or general beauty and excellence with the sword of Old Japan.

I crossed the long Shi-jo bridge after dark. The scene was very animated. Far and near the shallow river and river-bed were covered with little platforms adjoining tea-houses on the banks. Each had two or three Chinese lanterns swaying in the breeze; every one was the scene of gentle revelry; sounds of music and song and laughter echoed and re-echoed on every side. To spend these warm summer evenings over a cool stream of running water, in congenial company of friends and singing girls; to guess riddles, to make jests, to play noisy games, to sing snatches of love ditties, and to drink unlimited libations of *saké*,—these appear the favourite diversions of the youth of this great capital. One must not forget, however, that the students poring over books are neither seen nor heard, but only the revellers. I have known careless sightseers to draw sweeping generalizations respecting the frivolity of the French, from a visit to the "Jardin Mabille," ignoring completely the Latin quarter. Amusement more intellectual is possible; and on the other hand, pastimes far more degrading and brutal might be imported from the customs of Western nations.

CHAPTER XVI.

NARA AND KO-YA-SAN.

An inland excursion—Tea plantations—A stray Chinaman—Midnight alarms—Uji—Nara—An ancient city—A pagoda older than Westminster Abbey—The Dai-Butsu—The great bell—Votive offerings—A picture of terror—Saint Ko-bo Dai-shi—The holy mountain of Ko-ya-san—Hospitable monks.

September 5.—The prospects for travel hereafter are not very bright. "In June and September," says Murray's Handbook, "it is best to remain at home, for the continued downpour converts the roads into impassable sloughs, and envelopes the prospect in impenetrable clouds." But my home is not Kioto, and obliged to "move on" somewhere, I shall run the risks. One might go by rail directly to Osaka, but I wish to see Nara, and thence make a pilgrimage to Ko-ya-san. The best prophecies sometimes fail, and the weather thus far in September has been charming.

For the past few days I have employed the same

jinrikisha-man, and he is so good-natured, stout, and faithful that I have engaged him at a yen a day to accompany me on this journey. My luggage has been reduced to still smaller limits; the large basket I sent off to Ozaka by the railway, to be kept until called for, retaining the smaller one, large enough to contain my blanket, overcoat, medicines, and only those other articles necessary for a week's absence. My larger handbag contains chiefly provisions, and whatever it is necessary to get at conveniently and readily during the day. After lunch we started off.

Passed in the suburbs of Kioto the monastery of To-fuku-ji, one of the five principal conventual establishments of the Zen sect, and stopped to visit it. What are the distinctive points of faith held by this offshoot of Buddhism? I doubt if few Japanese could inform me, unless they happened to be priests. It is quite an ancient sect, however, founded some six hundred years ago. The present buildings were erected in 1347, and are tolerably well preserved, the grounds by far the prettiest of any in Kioto; now comparatively deserted; no worshippers in the temple. To see the chief object of interest the gardener was obliged to go for keys, and in a few minutes I stood before the finest statue of Buddha I have yet seen—fifty feet high, with statues of the two goddesses, Kwannon and Miroku, on either side.

Leaving the highway, the road now passed upward,

and into the country. Tea plantations are numerous. I looked into the Shinto temple of Fuji-no-Mori, dedicated to the worship of the first historian, or collector of official annals of Japan, one Toneri Shiano, who died, I notice, *the same year* as the Venerable Bede, the first historian of England, A.D. 735. A curious pair of trees were to be seen in the temple grounds, one with trunk so old, worm-eaten, and decayed that it must have fallen to the ground, I should think, by its own weight, if it had not been supported and entwined about in the most singular manner by another younger and more vigorous trunk. I have never seen a better illustration of youth aiding decrepitude, and doubt not it is used to point many a moral. Both trees were in full leaf.

It was near sundown when I reached Uji, and concluded to go no further. Crossing the bridge over a good-sized river, found a large hotel on the other side, where I was given, for the first time in Japan, a room on the second floor. It was not infrequent to find inns of two stories—most of them in towns are such; but I have never seen one of three stories before. It was a corner room overlooking the river, and I congratulated myself on having an apartment so far above the ground that there would be no necessity for closing the blinds at night. A Chinaman occupied a room on the same floor, and shortly after my arrival paid me a visit, arrayed in his own national and peculiar garb. He was very inquisitive, wanted to know where I lived, and where I was going, and without invitation sat down and began smoking in the centre of my room. He would have it that I must be very rich—"*Anata*, takasan yen, *takasan!*" (You plenty money, *plenty!*), accompanying his insinuated assertion by half closing the hand. My coolie (who has transformed himself into an excellent body-servant), I think, intimated to him that his presence and smoking were not absolutely necessary to my enjoyment, for he took himself into the next room, and there romped with the house-maidens, catching them in his arms like a rude boy, despite their scratching and pulling at his "pig-tail." They call him "Nankin," and look upon him with ill-disguised contempt. Went downstairs after supper to get a drink of water, and stumbled into a sort of court-yard, where some girls were bathing; one entirely nude had just stepped from the bath. She was not so much abashed as myself, and all of them laughed heartily at my discomfiture after I had withdrawn.

Uji, September 6.—Slept under a mosquito net, with blinds open to the moonlight. About two o'clock in the morning I was awakened by some person passing through my room, and spoke to him. The man approached, lifted up the edge of the netting, and made a long explanation, not a word of which I could understand. Intimated that "to-morrow" I should be pleased to listen to him; but without acceding to the suggestion he went away and returned in a minute or two, with two blocks of wood, which he clapped together loudly enough to have awakened the entire village, while standing on my balcony, repeating the operation rhythmically for some minutes, and then returned to his own room. I cannot imagine his object in doing it, unless to frighten away demons or ghosts. But why my room instead of his own?[1]

There was a battle here at Uji bridge about seven centuries ago (1180), in which an aged general, Yorimasa, with but three hundred men, resisted an army of twenty thousand men sufficiently long to enable his prince to escape. Against such odds there could be but one result, and when "all was lost but honour," he and his few remaining followers retreated to the adjacent monastery of Bio-do-In, where they held the gates long enough to permit the aged general to commit suicide in due form. He was at that time seventy-five years old. The monastery is just in the outskirts of Uji. In the principal courtyard a weeping willow overhangs a stone monument, marking the place of suicide. For a general to run himself through the body rather than submit himself to be captured alive seems from the most ancient times to have been esteemed honourable among this people. It is a sentiment which extended also to common soldiers; and in this respect has no counterpart in history, except among the Jews at the time of Josephus.

[1] I have since been informed that he was probably a night watchman, who wished to notify thieves and robbers of his presence, should any happen to be about. It was the only time during my journey in Japan that such an incident happened.

Nara and Ko-ya-san.

The temple attached to this monastery is one of the oldest wooden buildings yet remaining in Japan, dating from 1052.

The road hence to Nara led through few villages, although many were visible on the hillside. In this district the peasants have the fashion of fixing a broad sun-umbrella at the end of a long bamboo pole, in such fashion that it shades them while drawing the water from their wells for irrigating. The wells are often so deep that the man himself is quite out of sight; the bucket regularly rises and falls like the piston of a steam engine, but without visible cause. Cotton is grown in this region; the shrub is very small, hardly more than eighteen inches high, and the yield from each bush seems very little as compared with the American product. An excellent idea in this part of Japan and in the city of Kioto itself is placing a pail of cold drinking water and a cup outside the house, for the use of thirsty passers-by. Lord Hartington, during debate on the opium question in Parliament, once spoke of the Japanese as a nation of hard drinkers. This is hardly correct. *In one hour's walk* in certain parts of London, Liverpool, or Manchester, I have seen more drunken men, more persons manifestly under the influence of alcohol, than I have noticed during the entire two months of my residence and travels in Japan.

Reached Nara just before noon, and after resting an hour for dinner, began exploring the town. It was the ancient capital of Japan from A.D. 709 to A.D. 784. How little we comprehend dates considered by themselves alone! To realize how long since Nara was a capital, one must remember that the first Saxon king of all England did not begin to reign until A.D. 827. Here is a pagoda of wood painted red, five stories high, almost perfectly preserved, yet it dates from the year A.D. 730, and is older than any Gothic cathedral in Europe. Close by, and adjoining a Buddhist temple, is an enormous pine tree. Long ago its spreading branches were held up by poles, and, as if instinct with reason, the tree concluded to spread rather than increase in height. Its lower branches project in every direction a hundred feet and more from the parent trunk; and at every interval of ten or fifteen feet their weight is supported by stout props. Tradition says that this tree was planted by none other than Ko-bo Dai-shi himself a thousand years ago, as a perpetual offering to the divinity of this temple.

A legend is as natural a growth as a plant or flower; and Japan is full of them. Just below the temple grounds is a large circular pond. A thousand years ago, when Nara was the seat of the empire, a beautiful girl attached to the court was secretly wooed by the mikado. Perhaps when yonder decrepit old pine tree was in the full greenness of youth it may have heard some whisperings of the old, old story. By-and-by new faces and other eyes were more attractive to the fickle prince, and so the forsaken Ophelia came secretly by night, and casting herself in this pond, was drowned. One reads nearly the same story nearly every week in London papers. Human nature has little changed.

The pond is full of tame fish and small turtles, who approach the banks in great numbers to be fed. Japanese women watch the approach of a pilgrim, and supply him with food to throw them, in form of cakes and curious little puff-balls, about two inches in diameter, but so light that they float like bubbles on the water. The efforts of the fish and turtles to seize them are an unfailing source of amusement to crowds of pilgrims; the balls are too large to swallow, and the fish, struggling together to get a bite, simply toss it out of the water. Then the turtles move so slowly as compared with the fishes, that they would seem almost never to get their share of food.

The chief "sight" of Nara is the great bronze Buddha, larger than the one at Kamakura, which most travellers stopping at Yokohama go to visit. They tell you it is fifty-three feet in height—the figure of Gautama, as usual seated on the lotus. It is not very ancient, however, only a little over three hundred years old; its predecessors, however, are more antique; the first dating from A.D. 749. The face is black and ugly, corresponding little to either the Mongolian or true Indian type. Near it hangs the huge bell, cast in A.D. 732, thirteen and a half feet high. It is exactly the same shape as the bells one sees to-day for sale at the ironmongers of Kioto, the upper third covered with little projecting knobs of metal in longitudinal rows. Eleven and a half centuries—with what a period in civilization this old bell is contemporaneous! Why, it was more than three centuries old when William the Conqueror fought at Hastings! A man standing by offered me a stout club. I struck the outer rim of the bell as he suggested; it was as clear and sonorous as if it were cast yesterday. Yet it has tolled the fate of innumerable kingdoms, and outlasted every dynasty that was in Europe when it was cast.

More interesting than anything else at Nara was a temple full of votive offerings to the goddess Kwannon, precisely in character and object similar to those seen in several churches in France and Italy. They consist of little pictures, executed sometimes very carefully and artistically, representing the occasions of extremity or danger wherein Kwannon, besought by prayer, interposed her aid. Sick children are brought by mothers to her shrine, and rays of healing are seen falling from the image upon them. A blind boy is led into the temple; the bright rays from Kwannon's image are supposed to have restored his sight. A fisherman's junk is wrecked and tossed in mid-ocean on a disabled craft; two or three half-starved wretches are seen clinging to the nearly submerged craft; one is in the attitude of prayer, and there, in the skies, stands the Goddess of Mercy

Nara and Ko-ya-san.

looking with pity on her devotee. One picture represents a heavy rock fallen on a man; neighbours try vainly to lift it; some wring their hands; one old woman, however, is seen praying to Kwannon, and that her aid was given this picture at her shrine abundantly testifies. Another scene illustrates the escape of a mad bull; it has kicked down its hut; everybody is rushing away; a mother with a child on her back prays to Kwannon as she flies for safety, and it is evident that a refuge was gained, or the picture would not as a thank-offering be here. The old Japanese faith in the gods and their pitying watchfulness over mankind was implicit, earnest, and undoubting; will the new imported philosophy which sneers at her religion as superstition, and talks about "prayer gauges," make her people happier or their morals purer? That is the question for the future.

September 7.—Slept fairly, disturbed only by pilgrims' chants, which lasted until a late hour last night and began early this morning. The hotel bill when presented showed evidence of my karuma-man's thoughtful interest; it consisted of two charges, one for lodging and another for food—as if I were ignorant of the fact that the *hatago*, or charge made at inns, always includes both supper and breakfast. At Kioto, where I had an entire floor to myself, a separate charge was made; and this fact probably my guide ascertained, as he was present when I paid the last account. Of course in country districts and for ordinary accommodation the same custom would be simply a "squeeze," and I vigorously protested, showing bills of previous inns, and finally he struck off the extra charge. But it was singular to see him immediately turn to the coolie, and in my presence dun him for more money on his own account. "Anata, moto" (you, more), were plainly significant of a previous understanding. I am sorry to disappoint my man in such a trifle, but really he must let me make it up to him at the end of the journey.

Our morning's route from Nara toward Ko-ya-san lay along a perfectly level plain, rice-fields on either side, each with its well, quite deep; the water-drawer, standing on a platform halfway down, invisible to passers on the highway. We passed one well near the roadside; a young wife had brought her husband his second breakfast, and, the meal finished, she was watching him at his work. She was a timid little thing, and evidently felt relieved when the foreigner had gone on.

About noon it began to rain, and delayed progress for a couple of hours. The road now became more steep; we were climbing into the hills. Riding in the karuma was impossible, the stout coolie finding it quite enough to pull the empty vehicle. Our road led into a valley, which gradually contracted into a pass. Many villages or little hamlets, all thrifty looking and neat. Sundown found us at a little village a few miles from Hashimoto, and a comfortable-looking inn, offering good prospects of accommodation, decided me to go no further.

Nara and Ko-ya-san. 217

September 8.—The bed was a little harder than usual; and yet before coming to Japan I should never have thought one could sleep on a floor for a month with only an overcoat for a pillow! The sky at starting was overcast and threatening, but by nine o'clock it cleared up and the day was as warm as one could wish. The way was gradually upwards, and the road bad, stony, and steep. In many of the villages one heard the shuttle flying through the web, and looking through the open window, one was sure to find the weaver some young girl, always singing at her work. Every girl who finds herself discovered hastens to draw her garment over her pretty shoulders. The standard of feminine beauty is much higher than in Northern Japan. Turning a corner in one village, I came suddenly upon a little maid of sixteen—a veritable Rebecca at the well—nude to the waist, fair skin, and with very pleasing features; indeed, her smile as she gave me a bamboo-cup of water was bewitching enough to have won the heart of any Jacob in search for a wife.

We reached Hashimoto about ten o'clock; one crosses a river by a ferry-boat from the town of Gofo, a prosperous-looking place, through which we drove without stopping. Here my karuma-man said it was necessary to leave the vehicle, our progress henceforward being on foot. Left most of my luggage in charge of the landlord of the inn, my man transforming himself into a carrier, bearing on his back my blankets, etc., and provisions for a day or two. It was quite a mistake, however, to have left my things at Hashimoto, since the road was quite level and good for at least three miles beyond or to the next town of Kaburo, to which place the karuma might just as well have been taken. But the guide, I think, did not know it; from his frequent questions to passers-by, I fancy he never before came to Ko-ya-san.

Then I made another mistake. Not feeling inclined for dinner at eleven o'clock, I went through Kaburo, expecting to find tea-houses all along the route, as elsewhere in my travels. The result was that it was after two o'clock before I could get anything to eat. The road was very steep and rugged, climbed apparently only by pilgrims. Now and then resting-places were found, where excellent water-melons were to be had, refreshing but not particularly sustaining; and not a single tea-house or inn was reached for a distance that took us nearly three hours to accomplish. As the day was very warm, the journey was very tiresome after once the craving for food began to be felt.

The few inhabitants that live in this region seem rarely to have seen foreigners. Slowly climbing upward at one point, I stopped a moment for a breathing time, just as a lad of thirteen or fourteen years came in sight around a corner. The apparition of such an object in these solitudes seemed to startle him; he stopped, apparently frightened, although I motioned for him to come on. The guide was some distance behind and could lend no encouragement. The poor boy apparently debated in his mind whether to turn back up the hill—in which case I should be apparently pursuing him—or to make a bold dash for life and liberty; he decided finally on the latter course, clenched his teeth, and with the wildest, most frightened look, dashed by me down the hill. I could think of nothing so much resembling the action as the dash of a dog or cat when cornered and fearful of being hit or caught.

Somewhat further on I encountered a little girl, eight or ten years old, evidently belonging to the better class, carrying a large sunshade. The child was much frightened, but with sober courtesy, very pretty to see, made me a profound curtsy, which I returned by a low bow. Advancing a few steps she made another reverence, which I returned with equal formality; and she passed on, evidently rejoicing much not to have been devoured outright.

We reached Kami-yas about half-past two, well tired out. The place is merely a collection of inns and tea-houses for passing pilgrims, but the accommodation given me was so excellent that I concluded to go no further on my pilgrimage to-day.

September 9.—Shortly after sunrise, in company with a band of white-robed pilgrims with staffs and tinkling bells, we set out for the two hours' journey that yet remained. Seldom have I ever seen a more precipitous or rougher path; no cart of the crudest kind was possible as a conveyance. It is a mountain trail winding about in a wilderness of torrents and lofty trees. Such as it is now, however, it has remained for a thousand years, the path to the holy mountain of Ko-ya-san. No one but a hermit, seeking seclusion from mankind, would have penetrated an unbroken wilderness to this height; nothing but religious fervour would have worn out these stones by the tired feet of countless multitudes.

We pushed upwards, steadily climbing for two hours. Then the path expanded into a road; trees gave way to open spaces, until at last we reached the broad but uneven plateau whereon lie the temples and monasteries which make up the place. There are no inns, but at the house of a hospitable priest we were kindly received and made welcome to more than inns can give.

It is not difficult for one who has learned to love Religion for her own sake to become interested in what moves the hearts of multitudes of his fellow-men. Faith is not always necessary for admiration, nor even for reverence. Why have pilgrims flocked hither year after year for a thousand years? Because a recluse came here to meditate, and because this wilderness holds his tomb.

In the year 774 of our era there was born a child by whose posthumous designation, Ko-bo Dai-shi, or "Great Teacher who spreads abroad the Law," he is known throughout Japan. Of his childhood we know little; legends, of course, cluster about his early life.

Nara and Ko-ya-san.

We are told that he was conceived miraculously, and that he came into the world with hands folded in the attitude of prayer. At the age of twelve his parents sent him to Kioto to be educated as a priest, and before he was twenty-one he had attained the highest rank in the Buddhist priesthood. In 804 he went to China, and there received new enlightenment from a Buddhist priest, who was the sole depository of certain mystical doctrines transmitted from India. Returning home to Japan, he was honoured by being made the abbot of the To-ji monastery. It is said that on one occasion, while discoursing at the palace of the mikado on the doctrine of the incarnation of Buddha, some dispute arose in regard to new dogmas which he had introduced from his Chinese teacher. Turning away from them, he made the sign of "wisdom" with his hand, and immediately his face was observed to shine with an exceeding brightness, so that the emperor and his courtiers and disputing priests bowed to the ground in reverence as before divinity itself. In the year 816 he begged of the mikado the grant of this mountain plateau, whereon to found a sanctuary for meditation; he had discovered this place during his youthful wanderings before his voyage to China. Here, it is said, he had been tempted by fiendish visitants from the unseen world; visions which one of his European biographers ascribes to a "disordered nervous system, the result of exposure, fasting, and intense absorption in the contemplation of abstractions"! Some time, doubtless, we shall find his miracles thus explained away; but to-day at least not one of these Japanese pilgrims has a doubt that he brought water from a rock and rain from the skies, that he healed the sick without medicines, and stopped by his prayers the spread of pestilence.

The final scene of the saint's earthly life took place here on Ko-ya-san. He was sixty years old. Some months previous he had gathered his followers around him, and predicted that on a certain day he should leave them for ever. The day came, and they assembled about him; he addressed them, and then sank into a state of profound meditation. His eyes closed; but his looks were otherwise as of a man sleeping. In the same posture they carried him to the mausoleum, and when, a few days afterward, the tomb was opened, they found him sleeping, with complexion unchanged and hair grown longer. Out of this grew, perhaps, the yet prevalent faith that he did not die, but sleeps, like Barbarossa. Some seventy years later the mikado sent to the monastery a change of raiment for him, and the abbot again opened the tomb to present the gift. But the saint could no longer be seen. In tears the venerable abbot confessed the sins which probably obscured his eyes, and implored the manifestation of the saint's presence. After some time in ardent prayer, "like the moon issuing from the mist, or like a shape reflected in a mirror," came the vision of one whose garments were in rags and whose long hair had grown to the feet. Fearful, however, that others with less earnest faith might seek vainly for the sight of Ko-bo Dai-shi's face, the abbot ordered the tomb to be closed for ever.

I do not know a more solemn walk than the mile or more of path leading through the forest to the tomb of the saint. It is one long cemetery; an avenue bordered by monuments to some of the most illustrious of Japan's historic worthies. They are mostly fictitious tombs; the stone raised preserves the memory, but does not mark the spot of burial; it is supposed sufficient, however, to secure to those thus honoured the privilege of a new birth into the pure land of absolute bliss. Here are memorials to most of the mikados and shoguns; tablets to the boy Atsumori and his repentant slayer, whose story is one of the most touching in the annals of Japan. Nearly all were of the peculiar shape I have before noted—a cube, a sphere, a pyramid—one above the other, ending at the top in a cone. The guide pointed out the monument to a certain traitor, Akechi Mitsuhide, which is strangely split in two from top to bottom, as a supposed indication of Heaven's wrath. I am slightly suspicious of this marvel; a dark night and a heavy iron bar in the hands of a vigorous priest would produce wonderful results in signifying by broken monuments the scorn of Heaven for traitors.

Before reaching the mausoleum a little stream is crossed by a bridge, over which it is deemed no one unacceptable to Ko-bo Dai-shi can by any means pass. Some three centuries ago Hide-yoshi, having attained the highest position in the state through ruthless slaughter of his enemies, came to Ko-ya-san, to pay a formal visit at the tomb of the saint. But this bridge troubled him. Suppose that on the day appointed, surrounded by generals, priests, and princes, he their head should be unable to cross this bridge? There is a tradition that he surmounted the difficulty by a truly statesmanlike expedient. The night before the grand ceremony, accompanied by the high priest alone, the great general came as far as this bridge, crossed it without difficulty, and then went back to his quarters with a good conscience, satisfied that the slaughter he had made of his enemies was duly approved by the sleeping yet vigilant saint.

Beyond the bridge is the Hall of Ten Thousand Lamps, a wooden building perhaps a hundred feet long. Peering within the grated shutters, one sees only darkness made visible by little lamps. "No sacrifice," says a Buddhist writer, "can be more acceptable than a burning lamp," since, as he states, it signifies the wisdom through which alone Buddhaship is attained. It seems that in nearly every religion it is felt to be an appropriate offering. I remember seeing in the little dingy synagogue at Prague a lamp which had smoked in honour of Jehovah, for I am afraid to say how many centuries. The poverty of the temple does not permit

Nara and Ko-ya-san. 225

the perpetual burning of but a few out of the ten thousand; but these few even Parsees could not more faithfully have cherished and preserved; and for more than seven centuries lights have been here burning night and day.

Behind this temple is the mausoleum where rests the saint, not dead but sleeping. It is so surrounded by tall trees that one sees only a glimpse of the building here and there. Yet this glimpse seemed full of pious satisfaction to the crowds of pilgrims who kneel before it, that, which for many a long pilgrimage has been the one object of desire. But then reverence is a plant that sometimes grows best in obscurity.

There were several temples and other buildings, most magnificently decorated during an age when both wealth and faith more abounded in Japan than to-day. Guides conduct pilgrims about them, in groups of about a dozen, as the verger takes sightseers about Westminster Abbey. At one point we were all requested to go on our knees, and then at the other end of the building was pointed out a portrait of Ko-bo Dai-shi, painted from life, the eyes of which were done by the saint himself. Then began rubbing of hands, and sibilantly ejaculated invocations on the part of the pilgrims.

Returning to my room, I spent the close of the day in writing. My room was most charming, looking directly upon a little garden which appertained only to this apartment—a garden with rocks and ferns, a pond

Q

with gold-fish, a miniature stone bridge, and one or two shrines for certain deities. Just before sundown one of the monks brought in the bed; the two quilts, upper and under, were covered with silk, and above the bamboo-woven *makura*, or head-rest, was a scarlet pillow-mat of silk inwoven with the mikado's crest.

The intense stillness is the greatest charm. No noisy children or laughing hoidenish girls make disturbance in this sacred place. Twilight begins. The gold-fish in the little pond leap out of water, snapping at the insects which swarm about them. A water-rat stealthily creeps round the brink, and as frogs hasten to leap far out into the water at his approach, I suspect them as the prey he seeks. Presently a silvery tinkling as of many bells, faint at first and then more clearly heard, tells us that a band of belated pilgrims are entering the town. It is the hour of evening prayer, and from their own apartments the musical chanting of priests reaches mine. Then, as the moon takes early possession of the night, the deep, quivering tones of the great bell float upon the air; the peal is answered from the temple, and slowly, with melodious and far-echoing sound-waves, they alternately toll the curfew of the holy mountain.

CHAPTER XVII.

OZAKA.

Descent of Ko-ya-san—Travelling acrobats—Sakai—Ozaka—The "Take-shiki-ya"—The castle of Ozaka—Stones twenty feet long—A September cyclone—Hotel tied down—River scenes —American missionaries—Calling upon converts—A Christian service—Japan already more than half Christian.

Ozaka, September 10.—As at monasteries everywhere, no bill is presented to travellers; it is left to the generosity of the guest. Leaving at an early hour, we began the descent of the mountain. In rainy weather I have noticed the serviceability of the Japanese foot-gear, and as the path was slippery and muddy from a shower during the night, I stopped at a little shop at the entrance to the town and exchanged my leathern boots for cloth socks and straw sandals. The Japanese *tabi*, or socks, are made of blue cloth with double soles, the great toe separate, as in a mitten. The straw sandals were fastened on in complicated fashion, my guide assisting, and we started off. At the first steep descent their advantages were perceived, especially their security. Where a leathern sole would have almost certainly slipped, as upon a smooth rocky incline, the straw sandals seemed almost to grasp the stone, as a fly's foot might fasten to a window-pane. I never walked more easily in my life. Of course my feet were soon wet through, but that would have happened with half-worn European boots. Then, too, they are worn out by half a day's travel, but as a new pair costs but little over a furthing, the expense is not felt even by Japanese of the poorest class.

A JAPANESE GIRL.

We reached the town of Hashimoto, fourteen miles from Ko-ya-san, where the karuma had been left, in exactly four hours. The trip has been well worth the pains, but I should never advise a traveller to start out as I did, at mid-day, to make the upward journey.

My room at the inn, where we stayed an hour or two for dinner and rest, looked directly upon a field—here and there plum trees, and beyond, in the distance, mountains. Looking out of the window while at dinner, I saw a young Japanese girl, perhaps twelve or fourteen years old, standing under a tree and gazing at my barbarian personality with that innocent air of wonder and surprise that an English child might exhibit at the sight of a Hindu rajah or an African chief. I wonder if she ever saw a white man before? Travellers certainly cannot be very common; for in the month or more since I left Tokio I have not passed a single European or American.

About one o'clock we were off towards Ozaka. Had I known the difficulties of the road, I should certainly have hesitated about taking a karuma by the day, and I am very sure the man himself would have refused. The Kiimi pass over the hills was as bad a road as any on the Naka-sen-do; not only was riding impossible, but for much of the way I was obliged to hire an extra hand to push the empty karuma. The path downward was very steep. At one little village through which our route lay we met a travelling acrobat troupe; it consisted of a man and two little girls, ten or twelve years of age. The man beat a drum and directed the performance, the girls did the posturing. One of them, standing on her hands, bent her feet backward so that they crossed and interlocked under her chin, and in this position she walked about on the hands. The poor children looked half-starved; it was a pitiable sight.

The valley became wider as we progressed, and at the same time the signs of material prosperity were more numerous, the houses larger and better built. Reached Mikka-ichi toward sundown, and put up at the Nabe-ya inn. A new experience awaited me. One of the maids of the inn insisted in removing my worn-out straw sandals and the muddy socks, or *tabi*, and then another brought a foot-tub of hot water to wash the feet; services which I have usually performed for myself. My room was one of the prettiest I have had in all Japan. I tried in vain to copy the variegated patterns of open woodwork above the screens, but the patterns were too numerous and complicated.

How little idea of a country is gained by inspection of museums or collections of *bric-à-brac!* The Paris Exposition and others do not present realities; they convey only partial and therefore incorrect conceptions. The Queen Anne's house is not the ordinary mansion one meets in English towns; nor the Japanese house the average type of the cottages seen throughout the empire itself. You look in vain in a museum for the dress of the common people. You find plenty of jewelled snuff-boxes and pretty trifles of the aristocracy. How many English or American youths have ever seen a French sabot? Even a French artist, illustrating a certain periodical, desiring to introduce an American labourer in a picture of American life, represented a typical Yankee in *wooden shoes!* What we need is a museum like that at South Kensington, which shall present to us the simple, ordinary articles of daily life and daily use in Japan—the straw sandals, the blue *tabi* or socks, the wooden slippers or shoes, the grass rain-cloaks, the yanagi-gori trunks, the cloth garments, the interior decoration of actual dwellings;—these, and not merely the rare china, the grotesque bronzes, or the artistic handiwork made only for foreign markets, and seldom or never seen by the traveller through the country.

September 11.—It was raining at daybreak, but as it showed no signs of stopping, we set off notwithstanding. The road was pretty good; generally downhill. The rain was an autumnal shower, intermittent with bits of sunshine, and, of course, did not prevent peasants from working in their rice-fields. Approaching Sakai the valley widened, and the little rice patches became larger fields. Most of the irrigation, too, on a broad level is carried on by wells; and the bamboo-poles, by means of which water is drawn, were so thickly scattered over a wide area, that they suggested almost a hop plantation in Kent. The villages on a rainy day were, perhaps, seen to a disadvantage, and they were not pleasing. Several boys and girls I have noted, with fair complexions and features, quite European in type; but perhaps the explanation is not difficult, as we are nearing Ozaka. Passed a coolie carrying some vegetables to market at

Sakai; he lit his pipe with flint and steel and a bit of black tinder. I have not before seen this in use, as matches are made in the country and sold cheaply.

Sakai, a city of about forty thousand inhabitants, was reached about noon. Approached from the east it has a fine appearance, the numerous temples rising above the general uniform level of other houses. While at dinner a band of pilgrims entered the inn. The first to come in discovered me, and, instead of passing on, he stood opposite and whispered to each wayfarer as he passed by. Then the pilgrim would stare about him till his eyes met mine, and he had satisfied curiosity. Three centuries ago Sakai was the centre of one of the most flourishing Christian missions in all Japan.

Two hours' ride along a broad and level road brought me to Ozaka. There are one or two hotels where an imitation of foreign accommodation can be had; but I will have none of them while in Japan. Thanks to my friend Yangimoto, I had been furnished with the address of a quiet inn and restaurant in the southern part of the city, and to this we made our way by dint of many questions. As in Kioto, the approach to it is uninviting, being through narrow streets, chiefly occupied by singing girls; but one view from the window of the room decided me immediately in its favour.

Driving to the railway station, I found the baskets which I had sent by railway from Kioto, and which had been safely kept in store during my week's pilgrimage and travel about the country; to my surprise no charge was made for their storage. My coolie was well contented with two yen extra for "tea-money," and from this week's experience I far prefer for similar excursions taking a man all the way, to engaging conveyances from point to point. A coolie soon learns to understand your wants at an inn; and although they all try to "squeeze" a little, the amount can be made very insignificant. It is better, I think, to have it understood that the man pays his own expenses; in reality, of course, he endeavours to get these charged upon the traveller. As a rule I was charged only about threepence a day more than while travelling alone; an amount which, doubtless, went towards his own reckoning with the native host.

I have discovered by a map the precise locality of this inn; it appears to have been erected on a stone abutment projecting into the river Yodo-gawa, by means of which part of its waters are turned into a huge artificial canal, the Higashi Yoko-bori, one of the arteries of the city. The inn, "Take-shiki-ya" by name, is two stories in height. My room is an upper chamber and just at the corner which faces both up the river and across it. I doubt whether any house in Ozaka has a wider prospect or more charming view. The moon, which has just risen, is nearly at its full. In the middle of the river, here as wide as the Thames at Greenwich, seems to be a long flat sandbank, left by subsiding waters; of this artificial island several pleasure-parties have taken possession, so far as to moor their boats at its edge. The waving lights from innumerable boats glimmer on the water, sounds of laughter, mingled with notes of song and the music of guitar, fill the air, and on the island in the stream I can see laughing lovers and mirth-provoking maidens chasing one another in the moonlight.

September 12.—Rainy and disagreeable weather kept me at home during the forenoon. After lunch took karuma, and drove over to the foreign concession, hoping to find our consul, but he was not to be discovered. The great wealth which it was thought would accrue to foreigners by compelling Japan, sorely against her will, to open Ozaka to trade, was not realized, and most of the merchants have given up their business, leaving their houses for occupation by missionaries. I met, however, a young merchant, who gave me every information, and on hearing that I had just arrived, offered to be my guide in visiting the castle of Ozaka.

On reaching the outer gates, we found a few soldiers sitting in a guard-house, apparently without any officer, and to my companion's suggestions in Japanese a laughing refusal was made. " Come on," said my friend, turning away; "there's some difficulty, but we'll go on," which we proceeded to do, although the guard vehemently protested. It struck me as a somewhat irregular form of procedure, and I suggested as much to Mr. A——. "Oh, I always have some trouble with these fellows," he replied. "They wanted to send to the headquarters for a permission to enter, but I told them we would go for the permission ourselves; one doesn't want to be kept waiting for such a trifle." On reaching the headquarters some surprise was manifested by our appearance without the necessary permit, but another one, allowing us to visit the citadel, was granted without difficulty.

I have never seen a fortress whose strength chiefly depended upon art and not natural inaccessibility which gave an idea of greater strength than this castle at Ozaka. Of course others are vastly more impregnable— Gibraltar for instance, or Ehrenbreitstein on the Rhine; but to their strength nature has contributed quite as much as military science. Of castles or fortresses whose construction dates from the same period I know nothing in Europe to equal it. It is three centuries since Hideyoshi began its construction on the site occupied by a monastery, which, however, was itself strongly fortified; some of these works may belong to the earlier construction. Like the Pyramids, it was built by forced labour, and in the size of granite blocks of which it is composed even the Pyramids do not surpass it. The walls of the principal gate are formed by single stones; I believe the largest is *at least fifteen feet high and not less than twenty feet long*.[1] Granite blocks ten feet in thickness and twice

---

[1] Sir E. T. Reed estimates their size as considerably greater than this. They are certainly much larger than the stones shown in the wall at Jerusalem, or any that are visible in the Great Pyramid.

as long are piled one upon the other. Three lines of fortification, each with moat and drawbridges, are about the central castle, or rather the place where it stood; for, after lasting three centuries, the most magnificent building or palace in Japan was burnt, out of mere wantonness of defeat, during the revolution of 1868. The highest point within the castle commands an extensive view of Ozaka and the surrounding country, but there is little dissimilarity between the town as thus seen and the other great cities of Japan.

Returning to the outer gate, we found our way barred by soldiers and an officer, who demanded that we accompany him to the office of the colonel in charge. My companion professed great indignation, and was for pushing by the soldiers, but their bayonets were crossed, and he surrendered at discretion. One can't push by a bayonet when it is pointed towards you. We found an officer seated at a table busily writing; he was now on his own ground, and for a minute or two took no notice of his prisoners. Some words passed between my companion and this officer. I am afraid a little blustering was attempted, as "the only way to deal with these people;" but for once it had no effect on the commander. Our names and addresses were taken, and, after a vigorous protest, made in most forcible Japanese, we were permitted to depart.

My companion made light of the adventure, but I cannot help thinking we were guilty of great discourtesy to the military authorities. If Japanese gentlemen, visiting at Portsmouth or Chatham, had pushed by English soldiers, I very greatly doubt whether they would have escaped as easily; indeed, if they persisted in as utterly disregarding orders as we did, I am not sure that they would not be shot down. Yet fancy Englishmen or Americans equally offending, shot by Japanese soldiers! That is quite a different matter. Probably Japan would be given the instant alternative of war, or an enormous indemnity in gold, with the grant of a few more commercial privileges, thus far withheld, and the opening of new ports to foreign trade. Meantime, throughout Europe and America we congratulate ourselves that our ideas of justice and right are infinitely superior to those of other nations! But do not nations, as well as individuals, sometimes imitate the Pharisee in the temple?

September 14.—Went by rail to Kobe yesterday, to get letters and transact some business at the bank. On returning to Ozaka found a heavy gale blowing, which gradually increased to a typhoon; in fact, the wind was so strong that the coolie could hardly draw a karuma across the bridge. There was nothing to obstruct the full force of the hurricane down the river, and it was not pleasant, on going up to my room, to find the roof tied down by so many ropes that the place seemed like the deck of a ship. No doubt it was a prudent thing to do; at times the whole house shook and trembled from the gale, and it by no means seemed impossible for some particularly furious gust to sweep the whole structure from its foundations into the river.

I did not undress, but moved my bed near the door, and lay down prepared to get up in a hurry. It was a precaution of no use; for, despite the storm, I went to sleep, and when I awoke the wind had subsided.

Ozaka, I find, is almost as rectangular in its streets as Kioto. Numerous canals have made it resemble Venice in the number of its bridges, and the amount of traffic and transport carried on by these waterways. The two principal temples, the Higashi-Hon-gwan-ji and Nishi-Hon-gwan-ji, are in the heart of the city, surrounded by walls of massive masonry. The interiors of both are very fine, reminding one of the best Kioto types of temple decoration. They are not old, however; the former dates from 1615—say, five years before the pilgrims settled in New England—while the latter was built as recently as 1724. In the open courtyard of an afternoon children gather to play about the porches and on the steps, women with younger babes watching them meantime; a scene that suggests the little parks about so many of the Parisian churches, and their occupants on sunny afternoons. A great desideratum of Japanese cities would seem to be public parks; yet, after all, the need is not so pressing here, where every house has its garden.

The river this afternoon is very high and swollen. The island over which the lovers chased each other two or three evenings back has disappeared, and a fleet of fishing boats are anchored just above it. Their method of fishing is quite ingenious. Two bamboos, twelve or fifteen feet long, are fastened across a fishing boat somewhat in the shape of an immense V, a net being adjusted between the two arms, balanced by a weight at the point of union. The whole contrivance is so arranged that the net can be lowered like a large scoop into the water and raised at will. Lowered thus, with the two bamboo poles pointing up-stream, any fish swimming downward with the current would, if they passed between the outspread poles, go directly into the scoop-net. The fishermen were not particularly fortunate, for, after steadfastly raising and lowering their nets at intervals of five minutes for an hour or two, the whole fleet pulled up anchors and sailed down the river.

The current is very strong and swift; only by the most strenuous exertions are the peasants able to push their rude craft against it and up the river. The canal is full of boats trying to work their way out against the foaming torrent, which sweeps round the base of the promontory on which this house is built. Sometimes they creep along the bank, catching here and there at projections from the shore, and so pulling their boats up-stream. As I write, an accident has happened. A craft, which with difficulty had worked its way up the river a quarter of a mile, was in some way caught in the bridge, Ten-jin Bashi, and overturned. All the cargo of buckets and baskets came swimming down stream, with the empty boat, bottom upwards, accompanying. A broad coolie-hat, floating like a saucer among them, suggests that the owner went into the water with his cargo; but he is not to be seen, and probably was picked up by another navigator. Everything, instead of going down the main branch of the river, was caught in the current which sweeps past the base of this building into the canal. The boat struck one of the piles supporting the bridge, so that it stuck "amidships," and was broken in two by the force of the current at either end as I stood looking on. If it had struck the bridge otherwise than in the centre, of course it would have whirled round and gone on, perhaps unharmed; as it is, it was broken, as one breaks a stick across his knee, by the force of the current alone. There will be one sorrowful man in Ozaka to-night. "Why are the gods so angry at me?" perhaps he asks. Maybe before building or buying a new boat, it would be well to appease them by a pious pilgrimage.

September 15.—On going out this afternoon, I chanced upon an honest-looking old fellow with a new karuma, and asked him what he charged by the hour. His reply was not quite intelligible. "Did you say eight sen?" I asked, preparing to engage him at that rate. "No," said the honest old man, little versed in guile; "I said *six* sen," which is the usual fare for a Japanese passenger. I dare say he never carried a foreigner before, he was so polite, and trotted along so slowly. Yangimoto tells me that the higher charge demanded from foreigners is not altogether an extortion, but due to better service rendered; a coolie expects to go faster. I am afraid that this good soul, with his new karuma, was a novice in the business, for he went as slowly as if he had a Japanese fare.

Called upon two American missionaries living in the "foreign concession." Mr. C—— offered to accompany me to a temple in the vicinity not usually visited. I found it not dissimilar to some others I have seen, except in one peculiarity, the great number of votive offerings hung up in various parts of the building. Most of them were pictures, and they indicated, I was told, sometimes vows and sometimes prayers. A gambler was represented as breaking up his dice and implements of gambling, a rejoicing wife standing by his side; it was the public registration of a vow to break off the practice. Another picture was of a *saké* bowl, with a sort of padlock upon it; a prayer that an appetite might be restrained. A third picture, and one quite frequently repeated, was the symbol used to denote a *heart locked;* some too-fond lover prayed that the mistress of his affections might remain for ever constant to him alone. Egotist!

After dinner Mr. D—— invited me to call with him upon some native Christian converts. One was a physician, a middle-aged gentleman, very rich, who received us with great courtesy in his beautiful house.

Of course conversation, by means of an interpreter, was anything but animated, but we were both interested in each other's views on certain medical subjects. We then drove to the house of a wealthy tradesman, whose occupation is the furnishing of theatrical costumes. In Japan, actors do not own their own wardrobes, as for many representations they would be far too expensive, and so the business has grown up of making these costumes and hiring them out when desired. On arriving at the house, the owner most kindly offered to show us some very rich and curious antique costumes, now rarely used except on great occasions. While he was getting them out and ordering his attendants hither and thither, we were shown into a back parlour, where a curious sight met our eyes. His wife, a very beautiful young woman, was engaged with her friends in studying the Bible, assisted by a native preacher, a blind man. She received us with gentle and graceful courtesy, but excused herself from conversation on account of her occupation. They were studying the story of the Crucifixion, now reading and comparing the various accounts, now questioning as to facts or doctrines, and showing the utmost interest in the subject. From this we were called to a view of the costumes, silken stuffs heavy with embroidery in gold and silver thread; everything of the costliest materials. The owner brought out his treasures without stint, and seemed greatly to enjoy our admiration of them.

We next visited a school for Japanese girls, owned and controlled by Japanese Christians. Each little damsel has a tiny room, filled up with screens and mats. There is no attempt to accustom them to European luxuries in the way of chairs and spring-beds, which, of course, they could not have in after life. I was too late to see the school in session, but we saw many of the pupils. Notwithstanding the objections to such institutions suggested by Miss Bird, I cannot but think them productive of great good.

Going thus about the city, from house to house of believers, stopping now and then to speak to one in a shop, another on the street, a third working as a carpenter, I am reminded of what the earliest Christian churches must have been, in Rome for instance, where Paul lived in his own hired house and worked and preached. Now, as then, it is a little band of believers in strange doctrines, surrounded by great multitudes who hold them in contempt. One great difference exists—there is no danger in the profession of Christianity to-day.

September 17.—Have spent the day making purchases, mostly of *bric à-brac*, bronze images of Buddha, and wooden images of Kwannon, old armour, paintings on silk, together with articles of daily use. Mr. M——, a young Japanese gentleman recommended by the missionaries, was with me part of the time, but, without the least disparagement to his integrity, I can certainly

A STREET IN OZAKA.

do far better alone. "Squeezing" is so uniform a practice here, that he cannot help being suspected as an introducer who will return for his commission, and higher prices are accordingly expected. If alone, one can get at the actual value of an article much more certainly.

Visited one or two of the principal mercers or cloth-merchants for the materials of Japanese dresses. The assistants or clerks sit on the low counter, all in a row, each with his pipe and bowl of charcoal. A buyer enters, and each clerk, anxious for his custom, seductively smiles, pushing forward his brazier of live coals as an invitation to sit down and take a preliminary pipe before business. You seat yourself and announce your requirements. The draper calls in drawling monotones to a group of little boys, who respond " ha-ee " in a shrill, long-drawn chorus, one of them approaching for orders. The goods are then brought from distant shelves. Each piece of dress goods contains just sufficient for one gown, be it for man or woman; one would think people all of the same size here in Japan. Making and trimming is probably cheaper here than in any other country in the world where there is any making done. A man's dress is made up for fourteen sen, less than fivepence; a woman's dress costs a little more if there be much trimming. Of course this refers to garments for everyday wear, and of cotton, not silk.

September 20.—It has rained the past day or two about half of the time; in such weather one finds the city far more pleasant than the finest country excursions. This morning, about eleven, took a karuma and visited several temples in the outskirts, built on an eminence overlooking the greater part of the city. One of them is dedicated to the worship of a certain emperor, who lived about fifteen hundred years ago, and of whom a pretty legend has been handed down. Having ascended a hill one morning, he noticed that no smoke could be seen arising from the cottages, and on inquiring the cause, was told that it was due to the poverty of the people, which made it impossible for them to afford fuel for purposes of warmth. Returning home, he decreed that for the space of three years no taxes or forced labour should be imposed; his own palace, from emptiness of the exchequer, becoming so dilapidated that the roof admitted the rain. At the end of three years he again climbed the hill, and beheld smoke arising from every dwelling. Now the people were rich enough to bear the necessary imposts, and of their own accord contributed to rebuilding his palace. It is a story of patriarchal days, probably a fable, and yet possibly with some element of truth. The mikado's palace—even the one in which he resided as lately as 1868—might easily become dilapidated and admit rain, for the roof is thatched with bark or straw. There is a sound principle of political economy in the legend.

Mr. Yangimoto called on me to-day, bringing another Japanese gentleman. These two are all that are now living of a party of six Japanese students, whose acquaintance I made about 1871 when they first went abroad. One of their number was the nephew of the mikado, the Prince Adzuma Fushi-mi-no-miya, a youth who might have succeeded to the throne had the mikado died without children. I remember being impressed by the quiet dignity of the young prince, who displayed, however, even then the delicacy of constitution which foreshadowed his early death.

We spoke of Christianity. Mr. M—— thinks that converts come only from the very lowest class of society. On the other hand, Yangimoto believes the Government well disposed toward Christian missionaries, especially since it is seen that the new converts are good citizens, orderly in conduct, and in every way loyal. While he admits that converts are made from the well-to-do middle classes, he doubts whether any Government *employées* or members of the ruling class have been converted, which is quite probable. As a rule, religions do not first spread among the aristocracy; of old it was the "common people" who heard Him gladly.

And they hear of Him gladly yet. Mr. C——, the missionary, called this evening, and invited me to go with him to a native service in one of the suburbs of the city. We found a little chapel filled with Japanese working men, all seated on the floor, and listening most earnestly to the speaker; indeed, this intense eagerness of the audience was most striking. Mr. C——

went forward and took a seat on the floor in Japanese fashion, but I preferred a seat near the door, not being certain of my ability to remain in so constrained a posture for any length of time.

The preacher, an intelligent-looking young Japanese, spoke entirely without notes, and with an exceedingly impressive and earnest delivery. Prayer followed the sermon, during which the Christian part of the audience took the most respectful attitude possible, bending forward till the forehead touched the floor. Then the entire congregation sung a hymn, and the service closed. About half of the audience, I should think, were strangers, passers-by it may be, attracted out of curiosity. Many of them wore their hair in the ancient Japanese fashion, an indication of having withstood or ignored the influence of the foreigners. A more quiet, attentive, and respectful audience it would be hard to find in England or America.

"Our policy," said Mr. C——, as we walked homeward, "is to place the work as fast as possible in the hands of the Japanese themselves. The Roman Catholics, for instance, have the most native converts, but they keep the power in their own hands; they do not ordain native priests. The Greek Church, on the other hand, appoints natives to ecclesiastical positions, but being supported with Russian money, it naturally excites the jealousy of the people. Against us there is no such feeling. Just as soon as a small body of Christians, the merest nucleus of a church, can be gathered together, we ordain a native pastor, and ask them to support their church, leaving us to push into new fields. Mr. D——, for instance, starts to-morrow for a two days' journey into the interior, simply to marry a native minister and establish him in his work."

I have been greatly pleased with both these missionaries. They are hard workers and heartily in earnest. Each speaks the language fluently, and I note that they adopt in their intercourse with the Japanese all those little formalities of native etiquette, which perhaps as much as anything have won for them the good-will of the people. They say that no country can offer better prospects for the spread of Christianity than Japan at the present time; and I think it is true, for Japan is already more than half Christian in the gentleness of her national character and through the innate disposition to do right and deal honestly and justly. It was well that the spread of Christianity was not east into Asia, but westward; it was needed far more among the fierce nations of Europe. We know what Japan is to-day—"pagan" as we call her; but what the Celt or Saxon, the Norman and the Goth would be to-day if Christianity had not appeared among them, we can only faintly imagine by seeing how little the precepts of Jesus have lessened the inborn brutality of our national character; how slight the influence they even now exert upon our national conduct towards other and weaker races.

CHAPTER XVIII.

ON THE INLAND SEA.

A native steamboat—Night voyage—Primitive accommodation—"Boy!"—Okayama—The American mission—Call upon the governor—A Buddhist's praise of Christianity—A Japanese prison visited—On the Inland Sea—Islands and villages—Disembarking in darkness—A solitary sail—Unpleasant apprehensions—Night ride in a jinrikisha—Arrival at Hiroshima.

THE rainy season had now fairly begun; but a traveller whose time is limited cannot afford to wait for pleasant weather and sunny days. From Ozaka to Kobe and Hiogo is only about an hour's journey, and thence one can take passage by ocean steamer direct to Nagasaki through the Inland Sea. Although this was the more comfortable method of reaching the southern extremity of Japan, it seemed to me a mistake to push on so rapidly; and I concluded, therefore, to make my way by native steamboats and by land conveyance at least as far as Shimonoseki. Having learned, at the cost of much tribulation, how to live in Japan among the people,

On the Inland Sea. 251

it seemed a pity to shorten my experiences merely on account of a little stormy weather.

My friend, Mr. Yangimoto, had kindly secured for me passage by a boat which made daily voyages along the southern coast. It was nearly midnight when the coolie, previously engaged, came up to my room to announce the arrival of the vessel. There was little necessity for such notification; there she lay tossing on the waves but a few rods from shore, whistling and shrieking enough for a fleet. Pushing out from shore, in a few minutes I had reached her deck and made my way to the first cabin. It was crowded with passengers of the better class, nearly all asleep, or trying to sleep, amid the din and noise overhead. It was in vain to look for state-room or berth; as usual, one had to accommodate himself to circumstances. My hand-bag was transformed into a sort of leathern pillow; and, wrapping myself in a travelling rug, I stretched myself out on the floor after the fashion of the other passengers. There were no Europeans on board; captain, engineer, pilot, crew, and passengers were all Japanese. As a rule, foreigners do not take kindly to these native steamboats. "Some day these fellows will forget something or other and blow up the whole concern," was the not very assuring forecast which I heard at Ozaka. Possibly; but, as a rule, I fancy such fears are as groundless in Japan as they would be, let us say, on the Mississippi.

On leaving the harbour, the little craft was at first

most uncomfortably tossed about by the waves. Then the solitary lamp which dimly lighted the saloon flickered and went out, leaving us in total darkness. Immediately on every side arose cries of "Boy! boy!" and the sleepy servant came in and relighted it. Japanese do not like sleeping in darkness, partly, I imagine, because of the insecurity of their rooms. The English word "boy" has become the general term for designating a servant everywhere in the East touched by English influence. It has probably passed from India to China, and thence to Japan. Nevertheless it seemed a little curious that Japanese gentlemen, travelling in their own country, should use an English word to summon one of their own countrymen.

Early the next morning we arrived off the coast opposite Okayama, where most of the passengers disembarked. Finding my way to the city, I secured good quarters in a native inn; and, after resting a while, made my way to the city hospital, where, if anywhere, one may always be certain to find somebody able to speak English, French, or German. Almost at the entrance I had the good fortune to meet the chief physician, Dr. Berry, who most cordially pressed upon me the hospitality of the American mission during my stay. Somehow I fancied that he could not quite comprehend how any one who had ever slept in a more comfortable fashion, could accustom himself to sleeping on the floor week after week.

As the guest of the missionaries, three pleasant days were devoted to Okayama; and for the first time in two months I enjoyed the luxury of a spring bed, and the use of knife and fork in place of chopsticks and spoons.

I confess I can hardly picture to myself lives of more blended usefulness and happiness than have fallen to the lot of these missionaries in this out-of-the-way corner of Japan. They knew each other years ago, while studying theology and preparing for the ministry; they had found wives inspired by the same enthusiasm for a life-work, the same desire to make known to heathen the "tidings of great joy," and thereby to snatch perishing souls from eternal fires. They lived in houses built under their own plans and superintendence, after the style and fashion of New England homes. They endured, it is true, a sort of banishment from their native land; but they had escaped, without knowing it, that despotic rule of the pulpit by the pews, inevitable at home. Here they found themselves welcomed and beloved by the gentle folk among whom they lived and laboured, regarded with appreciation and friendship by the higher classes, with respect and civility by all. Okayama, fortunately, is not yet open to the peculiar civilizing influences of foreign trade; and the teaching of the missionary is not here paralyzed by examples of European manners and morals, which he finds difficult to explain on the hypothesis of a higher and purer civilization. One may indeed question the truth of that dogma which consigns to everlasting torment millions ignorant of a Name; but of the value of mission work, in grafting Western civilization and social life into and upon an Oriental stock, there can be no doubt whatever.

We called one afternoon upon the governor of the province, and were received with ceremonious civility. Of course the usual compliments and felicitations, personal and international, took up much of the visit. It was especially pleasant, however, to have a Japanese official of high rank speak so cordially of foreigners and their work, and that, too, without any pretensions of attachment to their teaching or their creed.

"I am," he said, "of another religious belief, and I have no wish to change from the faith of my ancestors. It is good enough for me. But I have noticed that those of my countrymen who become Christians are still good citizens, not less obedient to the laws; sober, industrious, honest. If this new religion produces such results, I think it must be good. The Japanese people are not blind; we notice who come among us simply to get rich by trade, and return home again; and who come with unselfish aims, seeking only our benefit." On leaving, he gave me one of those autographic apothegms, which the Japanese love to transcribe from their classical writers and hang upon their walls. It was written in most classical Chinese—

> "The wise man does not fear slander;
> At the perfect fruit birds will always peck."

The following day I visited the provincial gaol, where were confined prisoners sentenced to various long terms of confinement, the majority being for an average of about seven years. Accustomed to the inspection of European and American prisons, this one seemed to me by no means a strong one; heavy bars of wood appeared to take the place of iron elsewhere, and English or American housebreakers would laugh at such barriers to freedom. We arrived just before the hour for dinner, and the convicts were sitting, Japanese fashion, on their heels in long rows, waiting for the bowls of food. Everything about the prison was bright, fresh, clean, and even cheerful. Certainly I never remember to have visited a penal establishment in any country so free from that peculiar prison odour—that indefinite, subtle, and awful stench which elsewhere appears to pervade aggregations of convict cells. Possibly it was due to the frequency of hot baths, which are probably allowed here as in the poorest homes of the country people.

The governor of the gaol was a young man of more than ordinary intelligence, and appeared almost painfully anxious to learn, not only the best theories of prison management and discipline, but also the most approved methods for reclaiming the criminal, and reconstituting him a member of society.

It was after sunset when I bade adieu to my hosts and set out from Okayama for my next port. Seated, or rather lying, on the clean mats of a flat-bottomed boat, we floated by moonlight down the river to the sea, and late at night caught again the little steamer plying along these shores. Following a somewhat restless night's voyage, came a long and delightful day. Soon after sunrise I was on deck, enjoying for the first time the scenery of the Inland Sea. More beautiful in many respects it is difficult to imagine; more charming, at any rate, I have never seen. It is a perfect archipelago. At times we seemed to be in a narrow lake with land on every side at no great distance; then, shortly, a channel between islands would appear, and soon the little steamer would be ploughing through it into open water. The sea was fortunately calm, and fishing-crafts were out in great numbers. Every few hours we arrived off some city or town, where a small fleet of skiffs or junks were in waiting to transfer passengers and their luggage to the shores; and then, with much blowing of the steam-whistle, we left behind us the picture of its quaint houses and terraced slopes, with stone steps leading to some shrine or temple on the hillside; and then more islands, more fishing villages—too insignificant for a steamboat's visits—and another city or town, with the same excitement and the same reception.

It was after ten o'clock at night when we came to anchor off Hiroshima, one of the most important cities on the southern coast. Engaging a boatman from among the craft in waiting for our arrival, I pushed off

for the land. The sky was overcast with clouds, the
night dark, the town appeared to be some miles distant,
and only now and then could a glimmer of light be
discerned on shore. The river seemed to be swollen
with recent rains, and progress against a swiftly flowing
outward current was probably of necessity very slow.
More unsatisfactory was the fact, that instead of making
for where the nearest landing-place should be, my boatman seemed to be poling and pushing up stream, and
that in darkness so black that I could but just discern
his figure. Other boats had vanished. Where was he
going? I asked him, but his reply was so diffuse in
words that I could make nothing of it. At such an
hour of night, alone on a river with one's property about
him, with a man whose face one cannot even see, and
whose language one cannot comprehend, unpleasant
thoughts are apt to suggest themselves. I thought,
for instance, how easy it would be for this heathen to
bring that long pole crashing in the darkness on the
skull of his passenger; then to rifle his pockets, and
finally to let a limp and soulless corpse glide into the
swollen and swift current outward to the sea! But if
he were going to do it why didn't he begin? Why all
this strenuous exertion in the darkness, this pushing his
craft up stream? I watched every movement. Presently,
far in the distance, I caught sight of a faint flickering
and moving light, the paper lantern of some belated
jinrikisha-man, making for the city. I hailed him. My

boatman pushed his skiff to shore as directed. In a few minutes I had transferred my belongings to a karuma, and paid off the gondolier. He was profuse in thanks; indeed, I fancy I paid him a trifle extra for not "doing it." Poor old heathen! In his honest, simple heart he never dreamed, I dare say, of the dark suspicion with which a passenger once, for a "bad quarter of an hour," regarded him!

Drawn by a single coolie along a solitary country path by a riverside, at eleven o'clock at night, was but little more inspiring, and I was not sorry, after nearly an hour's ride, to draw up before an inn, even though it was closed and fastened up for the night. After much knocking and shouting, the landlord was awakened, and admitted me, more graciously than a traveller arriving at that hour could expect to be received, and I was soon safe and sound in a pleasant room. Safe enough I had been all the while. One laughs at the fears of midnight when morning comes. These honest heathen never had a thought of doing me an injury. Happily, they never guessed, I hope, the wrong done them in the imagination of a timorous traveller.

CHAPTER XIX.

HIROSHIMA TO NAGASAKI.

About Hiroshima—Hospital and schools—Call from the governor —Excursion to Miyajima—Fifteen miles at a stretch—Antiquities and relics—Dinner and poetry—Longest jinrikisha journey—Shimonoseki—Scene of the bombardment—The story of a wrong—Opinion of Sir E. J. Reed, M.P.—Voyage to Nagasaki—Last day in Japan—Steamships coaled by children —Off for China.

THE morning following my late arrival I set out upon a tour of investigation, hoping also to find somebody able to speak a little English. At the city hospital I met a young physician who spoke German, and from him learned that one of the teachers of the High School was supposed to be proficient in my native tongue. Returning home after a morning's ramble about the streets, I found this young gentleman awaiting me at the inn. His English was marked with much deliberation, and had been chiefly acquired from books; but it was far better than my acquaintance with Japanese. To the pleasure of my visit there I am sure he contributed not a little.

Hiroshima is a city of nearly a hundred thousand inhabitants, well situated and prosperous; with a city hospital under charge of an educated physician, and public schools that would compare well with those of many cities in Europe and America. In the library of the High School are the latest scientific publications in German, French, and English, and attention was particularly drawn to well-thumbed volumes by Professors Huxley and Tyndall, and Herbert Spencer. Many young Japanese learn European languages sufficiently to read them with appreciation, even though they may not be able to speak a single sentence correctly.

The same afternoon the governor did me the honour to call at my hotel. I should have preferred it had he come in the bright silken robes of his own national costume, instead of arraying himself in the funereal blackness of a European garb. To entertain him, I sent out for a bottle of the best wine procurable, in which we drank to each other's health, to the prosperity of Japan, and continued national friendship of our respective countries. His libations were not deep, wherein he showed most excellent judgment, for I greatly questioned—when too late—whether the contents of that bottle had ever known vineyard or wine-cellar, notwithstanding its pretentious label. The

Hiroshima to Nagasaki.

governor was very gracious, and invited me to go on an expedition with an English-speaking interpreter to the famous island temple of Miyajima, one of the most ancient in Japan.

Starting early the following morning, our coolies at once fell into a rapid and steady trot, never once halting for rest for the whole fifteen miles to Ogata! It seemed to me an extraordinary performance; but the fellows were young and strong, and the road following the coast was almost a perfect level. From Ogata we floated across to the island-shrine in a sailing vessel, whereof the sails were simply strips of matting unconnected except at the ends.

The natural beauty of the place is very striking. For more than thirteen hundred years it has been a Shinto shrine, and in its great temple still are kept souvenirs of great value to the future antiquarian of Japan. We were shown with reverence relics of saints, conquerors, and rulers—a letter from one, the sword of another, the votive offering of a third, all of which would have been more to me had I been able to carry in mind the details of Japanese history. Of what interest is the original Magna Charta, shown in the British Museum, to a Chinese traveller, ignorant of the struggle of English barons with King John and the results of the royal concession? Indifference to the national records of races foreign to ourselves is natural; but the vandalism that springs from such ignorance I find it hard to forgive. Over the exquisite hieroglyphs of the tomb of Ti at Sakkara I lately saw, scratched with a chalky pebble in huge ungainly script, the name of "U. Grant Houston, Porkopolis, Kansas." What was the tomb of an Egyptian priest who lived and died four thousand years ago, that a tourist, fresh from the boundless prairies of the "Great West," should regard it with special interest, or hesitate to deface it with his plebeian name? The greatness of some nations is undoubtedly in their future; even the New Zealander by the ruins of London Bridge is not the dream of an impossibility. It is a pity, nevertheless, when the arrogance of a yet unrealized ideal is permitted to obliterate the reverence that belongs of right to a great historic past.

The evening before leaving Hiroshima the principal teachers and officials of the town gave me a dinner. Perhaps the most interesting reminder of the occasion which I carried away was a series of little poems, all original, written at the spur of the moment under the inspiration of *saké*; all, I dare say, most complimentary, but entirely in the classic language of Confucius.

At daybreak of an October morning, in a karuma drawn by two coolies, I left Hiroshima with the intention, if possible, of breaking the record. It was over a hundred miles to Shimonoseki, and if I should miss catching the steamer to Nagasaki, it would probably cause a delay of a week just at the season when I was most anxious to get on. Encouraged by the promise of

Hiroshima to Nagasaki.

extra pay, my two men set out with evident determination to do their best. The road for miles lay along the shores of the Inland Sea, with enchanting autumnal views of distant islands and winding coasts, through a succession of thriving and pleasant towns. When, an hour or two after sundown, we reached our destination, the two young men had trotted no less than fifty-seven miles.

The next day's journey was slower; the roads were steeper, and it was more frequently necessary for me to alight and walk. Then, as I drew nearer to Shimonoseki, the coolie whom I had engaged to take me there, say, for two yen, drew me about a third of the way, and sold his bargain to another man for half the price I had engaged to pay for the whole journey. To me it was of course a matter of indifference by whose muscles I reached my destination; and a fresh coolie is a decided improvement over one tired out. On the third morning after leaving Hiroshima we passed through the pleasant suburbs of the town of Shimonoseki, and drew up at a native inn overlooking the water.

The interest which attaches itself to the Straits of Shimonoseki is purely historical. The town itself, of perhaps ten thousand inhabitants, is well situated along the shore, but without noteworthy difference from others on the coast. In front of the inn one looked across that strait, here perhaps a mile wide, which separates the main land of Nippon from the largest of its island

A SOUTHERN JINRIKISHA

Hiroshima to Nagasaki. 265

dependencies. Shimonoseki, one might say, is the Cornwall of Japan, or rather its Penzance. If one could imagine the principality of Wales as an island lying to the south-west of England, divided from it by a narrow strait varying in width from half a mile to a mile—less even than the width of the Thames below Greenwich—he can understand the part of the country which was now reached. From first landing at Yokohama, I had travelled through various parts of the empire for over a thousand miles.

With an English-speaking official, I visited the scene of that bombardment of Shimonoseki, which, with its subsequent extortion of gold indemnity by four great Christian nations, is probably the most shameful chapter in the history of our relations with Japan. In 1863 an American steamer anchoring in this channel was warned off; refusing to go, was attacked, and escaped without substantial injury, except to the feelings of the officers.

Then the American minister ordered another vessel to attack the forts, but it got worsted in the attempt. Other vessels of other nations took up the quarrel, tempted the fortunes of war, and were duly attacked. The Japanese local government had closed this channel, as they undoubtedly had a perfect right to do. No European authority admits the right of foreign ships of war to come and go within a quarter of a mile of its own shores when ordered away.

But Japan was in the throes of civil war. Here was

a magnificent opportunity for extortion! United by a common greed, the representatives of England, France, Holland, and the United States joined their forces, bombarded and carried the forts, and then demanded from an already impoverished nation the sum of three million dollars! No British ship was in any way attacked; yet England's share of the plunder was six hundred and forty-five thousand dollars.

There are no words too strong for condemnation of this act of piracy, instigated solely by greed. Now that years have gone by, the affair is seen in its true light both by English and American authorities. "For the sake of trade and gain," says an American writer long resident in Japan, "the foreigner wreaked a vengeance as savage and unjust as any that shames the record of native warfare."[1]

Sir E. J. Reed, M.P., an authority certainly in naval matters, who visited Shimonoseki, speaks of the "extortion" connected with the affair, and adds, "The Shimonoseki demand *was entirely unjustifiable, and the money taken ought to be returned.*"[2] The United States have finally recognized the dishonesty of the transaction, and have returned their share of the plunder to Japan. Eventually, it may be hoped, the blundering errors of too zealous representatives may by other nations be repaired, by the only reparation that is ever possible—

[1] W. E. Griffis, "The Mikado's Empire," p. 135.
[2] Sir E. J. Reed, "Japan," vol. ii., p. 129.

the return of the gold. No lapse of years will transmute that wrong into right.

It was midnight, as usual, when the steamer for Nagasaki arrived at the Straits and anchored amid stream. My boatman had been previously engaged, so I had no difficulty in being put aboard, and was soon asleep. All the next day we were skirting the rocky coasts of Kiu-shiu and the smaller islands, that seem to have crumbled off from mountains and set up for themselves in mid-ocean. One such peak, jutting several hundred feet into the air, is pierced by a channel, through which a ship might sail. It is a sort of natural bridge, leading nowhere; or rather a triumphal arch, built in mid-ocean.

A little before sunset we passed the island of Pappenberg, and came to anchor in the harbour of Nagasaki, one of the most beautiful in the world. Landing by a native sampan, I took a karuma, and, passing by the European hotels, found the native town and a quiet inn. It was now three months since I first set foot in the mikado's empire, and all but about a fortnight had been spent exclusively among the people. The last day should not be an exception.

Calling at the steamship offices the following morning, I learned that a boat bound for Hongkong started the same evening, and passage was at once taken. Had not various considerations urged me onwards, it would have been pleasant to have lingered a while in Nagasaki, for the place seemed very attractive in itself, and from its associations. Here for many years the Dutch had their trading port, to which once a year a vessel was permitted to come and exchange commodities. Here Christianity was introduced by St. Francis Xavier; here it was apparently eradicated by persecuting methods then in vogue throughout Christian lands; here in our own time the traces of its teachings and ceremonies have again been discovered, transmitted in secrecy from generation to generation for over two hundred years.

It was late in the afternoon of the 14th of October when my Japanese gondolier pushed his little boat through the waters of the spacious harbour, where the navy of a great nation might safely ride, and reached the steamer which was to carry me from these hospitable shores. Climbing on deck, the monotonous chant of children's voices indicated work of some kind; and, looking down on the opposite side from which passengers are taken on board, I saw that singular spectacle, a great steamship coaled by the hands of little girls! One by one, these children, apparently not above ten or twelve years old, took her basket containing a few handfuls of coal, and, carrying it up the gang-plank leading from the coal-barge, emptied it into the "chute" leading to the steamer's hold. The idea of coaling a steamer by pouring into it such an insignificant quantity at a time, seemed at first ridiculous; it ceases to surprise when one notes the steady continuity of the stream. It is the only method in vogue in Nagasaki. Even great war vessels are coaled by handfuls; but the many little hands are unceasingly at work.

The labour was nearly done. Already steam was hissing through the valves of our engines, as if the mighty force was impatient to be at work. The anchors were weighed. One by one the barges of the coaling fleet pushed away from our vessel. Fires were lighted under tea-kettles; some refreshment was to be had by the little workers even before they landed. A bell sounds; a tremor hardly perceptible shakes the ship; we are off for other lands. Of the people whom I had learned to appreciate so well, this, then, was to be my last glimpse—some little Nagasaki coaling-girls, blackened with dust, hungry and tired from a long day's work, yet singing and laughing as they floated at sunset toward their homes. Happier and healthier, even in such poverty, I am sure they are, under these skies, than thousands of their sisters who toil in the dark slums of London and New York, earning by their utmost endeavour barely enough to keep together body and soul.

CHAPTER XX.

THE PRESENT AND FUTURE OF JAPAN.

Statistics of population—Comparison with England—Death-rates—Physicians and hospitals—Marriage and divorce—Foreign residents—The work of the missionary—A laudable ignorance—Commercial ideals—European policy in the Orient—Lord Elgin on the war in China—The entanglement of Japan by treaty—Opinion of General Grant—His advice—The hope for the future.

THERE are a few facts in regard to Japan which are not usually deemed of sufficient interest to call for a traveller's record. Some of them depend for expression upon statistics; and the accuracy of statements implied by figures is usually unwelcome. Nevertheless, I venture to think that here and there they will find an interested reader. For most of them I am indebted to the work of Mr. Ishibashi, whose " Resumé Statistique " is a most remarkable compendium of facts relating to his country.

On January 1, 1886, the population of Japan was a

The Present and Future of Japan. 271

little more than that of the United Kingdom, according to the estimate of the Registrar-General.

	Males.	Females.	Persons.
United Kingdom (1886)	17,871,248	18,838,229	36,709,477
Japan (1886)	19,300,261	18,850,956	38,151,217

By the enumeration of December 31, 1889, the population of Japan was found to be just over forty millions. There is, of course, little or no emigration as compared with Great Britain. It will also be noticed that while the female element is in the majority throughout Europe, it is otherwise in Japan.

This population is scattered among 7,727,600 families or households. Subdivided as to rank, we find an aristocracy of 3825 nobles; a superior class, composed of the ancient military caste, or *Sammurai*, numbering not quite two millions; and a third class comprising not only the working class, but merchants, tradesmen, and artificers, amounting in the aggregate to over thirty-eight million souls.

Considering that a nation's annual death-rate is supposed to be intimately dependent upon the skill and learning of the medical profession, it is certainly surprising that in Japan it is only about twenty per thousand. This is somewhat higher than in England at the present day—thanks no doubt to the enforced sanitary improvements throughout this country; but it is less than our English death-rate twenty years ago. Nor do infants appear to be more specially marked by death in the

Orient than here. To a thousand living under five years of age the Japanese mortality in 1888 was 48. In England the average for ten years (1871–80) was 63. In London, however, this death-rate was 72 per thousand living; in Staffordshire, 71; in part of Yorkshire, 75; and in Lancashire, 82;—all of these districts showing a mortality of children vastly worse than obtained throughout Japan in 1888.[1] In other words, of a thousand children under five years of age the chances of death appear to be far greater in some parts of England than in Japan as a whole.

Of hospitals for reception and treatment of the sick there were 564. European methods of medical treatment are fast superseding the ancient reliance upon Chinese empiricism. Happily for Japan, she has escaped the medical dogmas which governed Europe for two hundred years, almost up to the middle of our century, and came to Europe for light when we had light to give her. Not only are the most untiring students in the medical schools of Europe, natives of Japan; but to Japanese physicians have been entrusted the lives and welfare of the London working class. Dr. Takaki Kanehiro, F.R.C.S., was at one time House-Physician in St. Thomas's Hospital. Sir Joseph Lister, in his introductory address at the London meeting of the International Congress of Hygiene and Demography, referred not only to the discoveries of Pasteur and Koch, but also

[1] See Sup. to 45th Ann. Rep. of Registrar-General, Table 3.

The Present and Future of Japan. 273

to those of Dr. Kitasato of Tokio, a worker in the same field.

It is, however, in the customs of marriage and divorce that we perceive the most striking differences between East and West. Under Japanese civilization it is expected that marriage shall be the lot of every woman reaching maturity, and in ordinarily good health. With most marriages there, as with us, contentment is undoubtedly the result. If, however, they fail to agree, separation ensues. Divorce is as easily accomplished as among the Jews of old. During three years (1884-1886), to each thousand marriages recorded, there were 396 registrations of divorce. It must be remembered, however, that in Japan, marriage is a relation, not a ceremony. In Paris alone, Dr. Bertillon estimated the existence of eighty thousand couples living together without the ceremonial approval of the State; but in Japan these would be marriages. Doubtless much of the ferment of unrest which leads to divorce is confined to certain classes. The great majority of homes are undisturbed. The annual proportion of divorces to existing marriages is but fifteen per thousand. Are we quite sure that under Western civilization there are not fifteen marriages in a thousand for which dissolution would be sought every year, if divorce were here as easily procurable as in the East?

Among the foreign nationalities which are represented, the Chinese naturally come first, 4975 being enumerated

T

in 1889. England stands next with 1701 residents, America follows with 899, while of Germans there were 550, of French 335, and about 500 of all other nationalities. These are scattered among the various open ports of the empire, and nowhere is the foreign colony very large.

But in Japan, as in India and China, exclusive of those attached to diplomatic service, the traveller is surprised to find himself in presence of two opposing camps of his own race. On the one hand are the missionaries, whose object is the conversion of the pagan to another creed. Over against them is the trading class, men whose compensation for temporary expatriation is the hoped-for acquisition of wealth. Behind the interests of commerce are the military and naval forces of the great Christian powers, and a diplomacy that has never hesitated at bloodshed for the promotion of Asiatic trade. Behind the missionary is only the zeal of religious interest at home and the force of moral ideas. In time of danger the two classes may coalesce; but certainly no greater surprise awaits the English or American traveller in Asia than he will experience while listening to the mutual opinions of each other, expressed by these two classes of his fellow-countrymen.

For instance, let me quote the impressions of a clergyman, the Rev. Theodore Williams, who lately visited Japan.

"Travellers in the East," he says, " often return with a prejudice against missions. This prejudice is strangely common in the mercantile and seafaring public, with whom globe-trotters are thrown. In the smoking-room of steamships, in the club-rooms of Yokohama, Shanghai, and Calcutta, the tone of conversation about missionaries is usually contemptuous. Such criticisms, for the most part, proceed from men incompetent to form a judgment upon a religious question—men who have no interest in the work of the Christian Church anywhere, who see Oriental life only on its worst side, and are themselves representatives of what is most gross, most disgusting, in European life. The foreign community in the East, as a class, exclusive of diplomatic and missionary circles, what does it consist of? Young commercial travellers, soldiers, sailors, adventurers of all nations. They are there for one purpose—to make money; are mostly bachelors, and go back to Europe or America as soon as they can afford it. Their views of Christianity are about as valuable as might be expressed in chance conversations at, let us say, Monaco. It is probably true all through the East that, of the many obstacles to the success of Christianity, the foreign colony, with its avarice, its sensuality, its brutal arrogance toward the native, is one of the greatest."

This is fairly representative of missionary opinion; and it must be confessed that its tone explains the existing antipathy. For hide it as we may, the missionary hinders the advance of trade wherever too great scrupulosity is undesirable.

In certain directions it has seemed to me that, as a class, missionaries in Asia were sometimes liable to form erroneous judgments of those about them, from what I venture to call a praiseworthy ignorance of sin. A young man, for instance, of exemplary life, saddened by the thought of the immortal souls daily plunged into everlasting perdition, determines to devote his life to their salvation. Arriving in India, China, or Japan, his eye is at once caught by every appearance of impropriety, every exhibition of vice, every deed of crime. "How quickly all this would disappear if the nation could be turned from its idols," is the natural reflection. From his utter ignorance of vice at home, and out of the very innocence of his heart, the missionary is liable at the outset to depreciate the people among whom he works. Take Japan, for instance. There is no vice there which does not more openly prevail in every great city of Europe or America. The missionary tells you of the Yoshiwara; he does not know the condition of the streets of Christian London and Glasgow. Of the nightly orgies on the Strand and in the Haymarket what has he ever seen? Of the horrors of Whitechapel lodging-houses what glimpse has he ever had? Why, compared with streets in San Francisco and Liverpool, the Yoshiwara of Tokio or Kioto is the apotheosis of decency. In all my journeys through the highways and bye-ways of Japan, I never saw such depths of degradation as I have seen in parts of London and New York.

The Present and Future of Japan. 277

This is not criticism of missions or missionaries. Ignorance of vice and sin is never discreditable, even though it leads sometimes to comparisons not quite just. It is the privilege of our century first to recognize that the sentiment of religion is not the unique possession of our race or creed, and that it may exist where once we had not deemed it possible. The teaching of Jesus Christ is not a failure. Even if there were not a single convert to be claimed, yet because Christian missions have tended to lift the world toward higher ideals; because Christian missionaries of every sect and creed have exemplified their teaching, not only in unselfish lives, but in outspoken protests against injustice and avarice; because again and again, everywhere throughout the East, they have stood between the oppressor and the oppressed,—they deserve well of history, when she makes up the record of those whose faithful work has aided the progress of humanity.

To what extent is there justice in the mission's criticism of the trading-class? It depends on the point of view. Granting every fact that is alleged against them as a class, nevertheless it seems to me that these young men who go out to Eastern ports are in all respects fairly representative of those in similar positions in London, Paris, or New York, neither better nor worse. They did not come to Asia for the sake of philanthropy, but only to gain wealth. With the creed of Christendom they have generally no quarrel; but the so-called principles of Christianity seem to them utterly impracticable as commercial axioms. To buy in the cheapest market and sell in the dearest; to crush rivalry, to push trade, to extend commerce, and to acquire wealth, these are ideals which every one can everywhere appreciate and comprehend. And if they imply something more; if trade invariably fights, first of all, for its own selfish interests; if it insists upon every exemption from responsibility, every unfair advantage once acquired, and standing, like Shylock, on its bond, would wreck even a nation's welfare if thereby it could touch gain;— why should we blame the trader when these are the sacred principles of every Government in Christendom? Is there a single great and powerful nation on the globe which even pretends to be guided in its treatment of weaker races by the teaching of Jesus Christ?

For it is one of the mysteries of life that in international affairs Christianity and "advanced statesmanship" are never in accord. Actions which no man of honour would for a moment approve as an individual, he does not hesitate to commend if they are the policy of his party or the measures of his Government. Even the very instruments of an aggressive policy do not always conceal their feeling against it. "Can I do anything to prevent England from calling down on herself God's curses for brutalities committed on a feeble Oriental race? Or are all my exertions only to result in extension of the area over which Englishmen are to exhibit how hollow and superficial are both their civilization and humanity? ... The tone of two or three men with mercantile houses in China is all for blood and massacre on a great scale." These are not the reflections of some pious and unknown missionary. They are the comments of Lord Elgin, while engaged in prosecuting a war against China, destined to result in yet more firmly fixing the opium trade upon a quarter of the human race. On another occasion he writes, "I have seldom, from a man or woman, since I came to the East, heard a sentence which was reconcilable with the hypothesis that Christianity had ever come into the world!" Even when he had arrived in front of Canton, and before giving orders for its bombardment, he writes thus to his wife: "I never was so ashamed of myself in my life! There we were, accumulating the means of destruction under the very eyes of about a million people, against whom they were to be employed. When we steamed up to Canton, and saw the banks covered with evidences of unrivalled industry, *I thought bitterly of those who for the most selfish objects are trampling underfoot this ancient civilization.*" [1]

If this were the spirit which then guided relations with the Orient, one ceases to wonder at the story of Japan. Over thirty years ago, beguiled by pleasant promises, and trusting, as we sometimes do in private life, to a sense of honour, which had been dulled by

[1] "Letters and Journals of Lord Elgin."

greed, Japan was bound hand and foot by commercial treaties which she not only did not comprehend, but of the full import of which it was intended she should be ignorant. At last she perceived her mistake. She had been lured into a surrender of one of the first principles of national existence. Taxation for the purposes of revenue, which every European nation without exception arranges to suit itself, was forced by foreign cunning to fall chiefly upon the poorest class in Japan, the cultivators of the soil. The poverty and distress of her people increased, until finally she asked for such revision of treaties as would merely restore to her that right of self-government of which so unfairly she had been deprived. This act of justice she has asked for years in vain. In the history of the last quarter of this century I do not know a sadder page than has been presented by Japan struggling bravely against financial embarrassments, educating her people into Western civilization, and yet slowly slipping toward that pit of debt which Christian nations have intentionally digged for her. More than once the story of her wrongs has evoked indignant protests from those who have visited her shores. One writer, many years a resident in Japan, says—

"There is no blacker page in history than the exactions and cruelties practised against Japan by the diplomatic representatives of the nations called Christian. . . . Of Japanese homes desolated, and innocent men and women torn by shells, and murdered by unjust bombardments, what reparation has been made, or what indemnity paid? For a land impoverished, for the miseries of a people compelled by foreigners to open their country for the sake of cursed dollars, what sympathy? For their defiling immorality, their brutal violence, their rum, what benefits have been given in return? Of real encouragement, of cheer to Japan in her mighty struggle, what word? Only the answer of the horse-leech, 'Blood! blood!' and at all times 'Gold! gold!' Is Heaven always on the side of the heaviest artillery?"[1]

But this, it may be said, is only the opinion of a civilian. Let us, then, see what was the impression of a soldier and a statesman. General U. S. Grant, under whom the civil war in America was brought to a close, and who was twice elected to the Presidency of the Republic, visited the East about a dozen years ago. He was no prejudiced critic. Of British rule in India, he says, "I do not see what could take its place but anarchy," and he speaks of what England has done for her Indian subjects in terms of abundant appreciation. "But since I left India," he adds, "I have seen things that made my blood boil in the way European powers attempt to degrade Asiatic nations. I did not believe such a policy possible. It seems to have no other aim than the extinction of their independence. It seems

[1] W. E. Griffis, "The Mikado's Empire," p. 377.

incredible that rights which we regard as essential to our national existence, and which no European nation, however small, would surrender, are denied to China and Japan. Among these rights none is so important as the right to control commerce. Japan especially seems to me in a position where the control of her commerce would enable her statesmen to relieve the people of their one great burden—the land tax, the effect of which is to impoverish them."[1]

But of more weight than any opinion are the changes which are steadily taking place in the distribution of the national wealth; changes which are beginning to cause serious apprehension among the intelligent portion of the Japanese people. A native writer has pointed out that capital is passing into the hands of a smaller number of individuals. "Land, for example, which in the eyes of a Japanese farmer is something more than mere property, something sacred, which he is bound to maintain as the legacy of his ancestors, *is rapidly being transferred from the ownership of small proprietors to the hands of richer men.*" The absolute proof of this statement is to be seen in the steady decrease of the number of persons registered by the Government as qualified for the right of suffrage. By payment of a land-tax of about a pound sterling the Japanese farmer is qualified to vote; by payment of a yet larger tax of about two pounds sterling, he becomes, under certain conditions, qualified

[1] Young's "Round the World with General Grant," p. 583.

for election to the general assemblies. *Now, both of these classes are steadily diminishing in number.* In 1880 the total number of duly qualified electors was 1,809,610; in 1888 these had decreased to 1,505,183, a falling-off of nearly seventeen per cent. ! The number of persons qualified to be elected were 879,347 in 1880. Eight years after, they had decreased to 803,795 ; a loss of 8½ per cent.

Coincident with this shifting of wealth-distribution, is the increase of pauperism. In 1882 the persons receiving public relief aggregated 6047. This number steadily increased to 15,204 in 1887, and 14,721 in 1888. Is an increasing impoverishment of the people the price Japan must needs pay for the introduction of European civilization? Is the tendency of modern society inevitably to make the few rich, and the masses poor? This was not what we found in Japan when we broke down the barriers of her seclusion. " A community entirely self-supporting ; peace within and without ; no want; no ill-will between classes ;—this is what I find in Japan in 1858, after one hundred years' exclusion of foreigners and foreign trade," wrote Lord Elgin thirty-four years ago. Across the mind of the far-seeing diplomatist flashed a fear that the civilization he was helping to force upon the Japanese might not be wholly a blessing ; that in opening their country to the West we were " bringing upon them misery and ruin." Happily, his generous fear has not yet been realized, but the tendency of present conditions cannot be mistaken. And if we ask why it is that, despite industry and thrift, the people of Japan are becoming poorer every day, there can be but one reply. It is because the greed of Christian Europe still refuses to a sister nation the act of justice which she asks; the revision of a commercial treaty which she made in ignorance, and by which she gave away her rights without compensation.

That any ultimate injury to British trade would follow that act of justice I do not believe; but it is probable that sordid fear in the minds of statesmen alone hinders the reparation that is asked. But with Japan this is more than a question of finance—it is a question of honour as well; and she will not always be under a duress to which Canada or Australia would not for a moment submit. It is impossible that the honour and interests of a nation of forty millions should be perpetually governed by a selfish policy at home, or subordinated to the preferences of a few hundred Europeans and Americans encamped on her soil. It was the opinion and advice of General Grant that Japan should make an appeal to the civilized world, pointing out the circumstances under which the treaty was made, explaining how her ignorance was skilfully used to place her in a position of dependence and humiliation; and that coincident with this appeal she should assume that full and complete sovereignty in respect to the management of her own affairs, of which so long and so unjustly

The Present and Future of Japan.

she has been deprived. "If," he said, "Japan would thus assert her rights, she would find that her cause would meet the approval of mankind." But thus speaks a soldier of Anglo-Saxon lineage who once commanded a million men; he forgot for a moment Shimonoseki and the bombardment of Canton. It seems to me that, guided by prudence, Japan has taken the wiser and safer course, of waiting for the awakening conscience of England to recognize the justice of her claim. Some day it will come; and therein one hope always remains to her. "For there is in England," said General Grant, "a widespread desire for justice and fair play, to which Japan need never appeal in vain." Let us trust he was right.

NOTE.

DURING three months' travel in Japan I slept but a few nights outside of native inns, and my own experience proved conclusively to myself the facility with which a traveller may reduce his luggage to very narrow limits, and without any extraordinary deprivation.

A dozen pots of Liebig's Extract lasted two months. Eggs and fish are generally procurable everywhere, particularly near the sea coast. Milk cannot be had in the interior. Saccharin is the best form of sweetening for tea or coffee; but a pound or two of loaf sugar will be very useful as presents to children. Tea is in universal use, but a first-class quality had best be carried if one is fond of it. Three or four tins of condensed coffee and chocolate are likely to be appreciated. Condiments should be taken according to taste; their space is insignificant. Biscuits, bread, jams, cheese, bacon, potted meats, and bottled beer I dispensed with, as adding bulk and weight to luggage without corresponding advantages. Two or three spoons were found necessary, but I had no use for knife and fork in the interior after learning to eat with chop-sticks. I mention all these solely for the traveller who desires to reduce his luggage to the lowest limits. Others, and especially those unaccustomed to the sacrifice of any comforts, had better take all they wish to eat and drink.

Of clothing, I advise two suits of flannels or serge, and flannel underwear. Murray's Guide-book (Satow and Hawes) states that washing cannot be done in the interior, and suggests the despatch home of linen by a forwarding company. I think this unnecessary for the average traveller. The Japanese understand perfectly how to wash all kinds of underwear; it is the subsequent mangling or ironing which is beyond them at present, and these refinements of civilization are about as necessary in Central Japan as with Stanley in Central Africa. Of course, this refers to country districts; one can get linen done up in all the large cities almost as well as at home.

www.ingramcontent.com/pod-product-compliance
Lightning Source LLC
Chambersburg PA
CBHW021958220426
43663CB00007B/870